JENNIFER LOPEZ

Recent Titles in Greenwood Biographies

JENNIFER LOPEZ

A Biography

Kathleen Tracy

GREENWOOD BIOGRAPHIES

GREENWOOD PRESS
WESTPORT, CONNECTICUT • LONDON

Library of Congress Cataloging-in-Publication Data

Tracy, Kathleen.
  Jennifer Lopez : a biography / Kathleen Tracy.
  p. cm. — (Greenwood biographies, ISSN 1540–4900)
  Includes bibliographical references and index.
  ISBN 978–0–313–35515–8 (alk. paper)
  1. Lopez, Jennifer, 1970– 2. Motion picture actors and actresses—United States—
Biography. 3. Singers—United States—Biography. I. Title.
  PN2287.L634T73 2008
  791.4302'8092—dc22
  [B] 2008020665

British Library Cataloguing in Publication Data is available.

Library of Congress Catalog Card Number: 2008020665
ISBN: 978–0–313–35515–8
ISSN: 1540–4900

First published in 2008

Greenwood Press, 88 Post Road West, Westport, CT 06881
An imprint of Greenwood Publishing Group, Inc.
www.greenwood.com

Printed in the United States of America

The paper used in this book complies with the
Permanent Paper Standard issued by the National
Information Standards Organization (Z39.48–1984).

10 9 8 7 6 5 4 3 2 1

CONTENTS

Photo essay follows page 60

SERIES FOREWORD

In response to high school and public library needs, Greenwood developed this distinguished series of full-length biographies specifically for student use. Prepared by field experts and professionals, these engaging biographies are tailored for high school students who need challenging yet accessible biographies. Ideal for secondary school assignments, the length, format and subject areas are designed to meet educators' requirements and students' interests.

Greenwood offers an extensive selection of biographies spanning all curriculum-related subject areas including social studies, the sciences, literature and the arts, history and politics, as well as popular culture, covering public figures and famous personalities from all time periods and backgrounds, both historic and contemporary, who have made an impact on American and/or world culture. Greenwood biographies were chosen based on comprehensive feedback from librarians and educators. Consideration was given to both curriculum relevance and inherent interest. The result is an intriguing mix of the well known and the unexpected, the saints and sinners from long-ago history and contemporary pop culture. Readers will find a wide array of subject choices from fascinating crime figures like Al Capone to inspiring pioneers like Margaret Mead, from the greatest minds of our time like Stephen Hawking to the most amazing success stories of our day like J. K. Rowling.

While the emphasis is on fact, not glorification, the books are meant to be fun to read. Each volume provides in-depth information about the subject's life from birth through childhood, the teen years, and adulthood. A thorough account relates family background and education, traces

personal and professional influences, and explores struggles, accomplish-
ments, and contributions. A timeline highlights the most significant life
events against a historical perspective. Bibliographies supplement the reference value of each volume.

INTRODUCTION

Jennifer Lopez was the right performer who came of age in the right time. Riding the wave of surging interest in all things Latin, Lopez first blazed into the spotlight when she starred in the 1997 film *Selena* playing the singer who herself was poised for crossover stardom when she was murdered by her obsessed former fan club president. The role transformed Lopez into a bona fide movie star. Since then, she has become one of Hollywood's highest paid actresses, a platinum-selling recording star, a successful TV and film producer, and the creative force behind her clothing line.

As most celebrities find out, the cost of stardom can be unexpectedly steep. Thanks to two short-lived marriages and some high-profile romances Lopez became a media magnet, with her every move and liaison followed in breathless detail. For a while Lopez seemed a veritable drama magnet. Whether Lopez was the victim of circumstance or the purveyor of her own personal soap opera was open for debate.

It is inarguable, though, that Jennifer Lopez blazed a trail no openly Latin actress had gone before. While Rita Hayworth and Raquel Welch enjoyed their own brand of stardom, mostly of the sex-symbol kind, neither woman proudly flaunted her heritage in their heyday. At the time they came onto the Hollywood scene, they were encouraged to cosmetically downplay their ethnicity and change their names to more Anglo-friendly *nom de plumes*. Lopez never considered hiding her heritage and as a result broke new ground into unprecedented territory with every career move she made.

In the beginning of her career Lopez found herself stuck in Hollywood-style stereotypic roles, such as the Melinda Lopez character on the television series *Second Chances* and *Hotel Malibu* in 1993–94. Today her roles are ethnic agnostic. Whether this is because the entertainment industry is finally opening more doors to minority actors or Lopez has just succeeded in knocking down doors in a way other Latin actress haven't been able to remains to be seen.

"If I could describe myself in a few words," Jennifer has said, "*strong* would be one of them. I know what I want, and I'm willing to go after it."[1]

NOTE

1. Veronica Chambers and John Leland. "Lovin' La Vida Loca." *Newsweek*, May 31, 1999, p. 72.

TIMELINE: EVENTS IN THE LIFE OF JENNIFER LOPEZ

July 24, 1970	Born in the Bronx, New York.
1975	Starts taking dance lessons.
1983	Attends Preston High School in the Bronx borough of New York City.
1986	Begins dating David Cruz.
1987	Graduates from Preston High.
	Enrolls at Baruch College in New York City but leaves after one semester.
	Makes film debut in *My Little Girl*, playing Myra.
1988	Leaves home and rents small apartment in New York City's Hell's Kitchen neighborhood.
	Tours Europe for five months with *Golden Musicals of Broadway* stage production.
	Tours Japan in a production of *Synchronicity*.
1989	Goes on her first commercial audition.
	Appears in regional productions of *Oklahoma* and *Jesus Christ Superstar*.
1991	Relocates to Los Angeles to appear on *In Living Color* as a Fly Girl.
1992	Hires Eric Gold to be her manager.
1993	Hired as dancer in Janet Jackson's "That's the Way Love Goes" music video.
	Plays Rosie Romero in TV movie *Nurses on the Line: The Crash of Flight 7*.
	Plays Melinda Lopez on the TV series *Second Chances*.

1994   Northridge earthquake shuts down *Second Chances* production.

Plays Melinda Lopez in the TV series *Hotel Malibu*.

Plays Lucy in the TV series *South Central*.

Co-hosts *Coming up Roses* on CBS.

1995   Plays Grace Santiago in *Money Train*.

Plays the young Maria in *My Family*.

Appears in a Coke commercial.

1996   Plays Gabriela in *Blood and Wine*.

Plays Miss Marquez in *Jack*.

Is cast as *Selena*.

Lopez becomes the highest paid Latina Hollywood actress earning $1 million for *Selena*.

Appears on cover of *Latina* magazine's premiere issue.

Ojani Noa proposes at the *Selena* wrap party in October.

1997   Marries Ojani Noa on February 22.

Gives *Movieline* interview that disses several A-list actresses.

Attends first Oscar ceremony in March.

Plays Grace McKenna in *U-Turn*.

People magazine names Lopez as one of the 50 Most Beautiful People in the World.

Plays Terri Flores in *Anaconda*.

Plays Selena Quintanilla-Pérez in *Selena*.

Lopez appears in Sean Combs's "Been Around the World" music video.

Signs spokesperson deal with L'Oreal.

1998   Separates from Noa in January.

Presents at the Oscars in March.

Divorces Noa in March.

Begins dating Sean Puffy Combs in March.

Severs relationship with her personal publicist Karynne Tencer.

Provides the voice of Azteca in the animated *Antz*.

Plays Karen Sisco in *Out of Sight*.

Details magazine names Lopez the Sexiest Woman of the Year.

Wins Outstanding Actress ALMA for *Selena*.

Earns Golden Globe nomination for *Selena*.

Appears in Marc Anthony's "*No me ames* (You Don't Love Me)" music video.

1999   Releases her first album, *On the 6*.

People again names Lopez one of the 50 Most Beautiful People in the World.

Wins Outstanding Actress in Crossover Role ALMA for *Out of Sight*.

Named Most Fashionable Female Artist at VH1/ Vogue Fashion Awards.

Story appears in *People* about Lopez being difficult on the set of *The Cell*.

Is taken into police custody along with Combs after a club shooting.

2000   Performs at the 27th annual American Music Awards in January.

Wears controversial green Versace dress at the Grammys.

Begins using the nickname J Lo.

Plays Catherine Deane in *The Cell*.

Wins Female Entertainer of the Year ALMA.

Releases *Let's Get Loud* CD.

Wins Favorite New Music Artist at Nickelodeon Kids' Choice Awards.

2001   Ends relationship with Combs in February.

Plays Mary Fiore in *The Wedding Planner*.

Attends Academy Awards with new boyfriend Cris Judd.

Plays Sharon Pogue in *Angel Eyes*.

Marries Cris Judd in September.

Jennifer's new clothing line debuts.

Wins MTV Movie Award for *The Cell*.

Wins ALMA's Female Entertainer of the Year Award.

Releases second album, *J. Lo*.

2002   Separates from Judd in June.

Files for divorce in August.

J to tha L-O!: The Remixes CD released.

Becomes engaged to Ben Affleck in November.

Plays Marisa Ventura *Maid in Manhattan*.

Plays Slim Hiller in *Enough*.

Releases *This is Me . . . Then* CD.

Nominated for two ALMA Awards.

Named ShoWest's Female Star of the Year.

Wins World's Best-Selling Latin Female Artist at the World Music Awards.

2003 Wins an American Music Award for Favorite Pop/Rock Female.

Plays Ricki in *Gigli*.

September wedding to Affleck postponed.

Wins American Music Awards for Favorite Pop/Rock Female Artist.

2004 Announces her split from Ben Affleck on January 20.

Plays Gertrude Steiney in *Jersey Girl*.

Plays Paulina in *Shall We Dance*.

Marries Marc Anthony in Beverly Hills on June 5.

2005 Plays Charlotte 'Charlie' Cantilini in *Monster-in-Law*.

Launches a new high-end clothing line, called Sweetface in February.

Plays Jean Gilkyson in *An Unfinished Life*.

Releases *Get Right* CD.

2006 Plays Lauren Adrian in *Bordertown*.

Plays Puchi in *El Cantante*.

Executive produces TV series *South Beach*.

Releases *Rebirth* CD.

Named Style Icon Of The Year Award.

Wins ACE Award for Accessories.

Is Honored with a Women in Film Crystal Award.

2007 Produces MTV reality series *Dance Life*.

Announces pregnancy in November.

Releases *Brave* CD.

2008 Earns four Billboard Latin Music Award nominations.

Gives birth to fraternal twins on February 22.

Chapter 1

BRONX BABY

To most people, "New York" means Manhattan. But that bustling metropolitan nerve center is only one of the five counties, called boroughs, which make up New York City. The other four are the Bronx, Brooklyn, Staten Island, and Queens. The five boroughs were separate entities up until 1889, at which point they were incorporated with Manhattan to form the New York City metropolis. Each of these boroughs has retained a distinctive personality that produces New Yorkers cut from very different cloths.

The Bronx, which is north of Queens and northeast of Manhattan, is a borough of contrasts. Around the turn of the nineteenth century, immigrant families from Europe and from tenements on Manhattan's Lower East Side moved to the Bronx where they found a more stable, upwardly mobile environment. Yet at the same time, the tree-lined Riverdale and Fieldston neighborhoods remained two of New York's most elegant regions. The borough also boasts many parks, including the New York Botanical Garden and the Wildlife Conservation Society, otherwise known as the Bronx Zoo.

But the well-heeled aspects of the borough were overshadowed by the destruction and devastation of the South Bronx. The crime and violence of the area in the 1960s and 1970s often left the police protecting the area feeling as if they were working in the middle of an enemy country. Beginning in the mid-1970s, the descendants of the families who had moved to the borough looking for a better life were fleeing the South Bronx for the suburbs as if running from a plague, leaving behind a poorer population and ghost neighborhoods. The Morrisania and Mott Haven sections of the South Bronx were estimated to have lost 150,000 residents during the decade. As more people left, arson, gangs, and drug dealers took over—in 1975 alone, there were over 13,000 fires set in one 12-square-mile area.[1]

With the economic spine of the area broken, the once-handsome neighborhood turned into a ghetto.

During Jimmy Carter's term as President in the late 1970s, he made an infamous visit to Charlotte Street in the Bronx, and camera crews accompanying the Chief Executive broadcast shocking footage of a war-like zone—burned-down buildings, abandoned neighborhoods, roving gangs of dead-eyed youths patrolling the ravaged streets. The South Bronx was a disaster of national proportions that became synonymous with inner-city blight everywhere in the nation and with the phenomenon called *white flight*, the large-scale exodus of middle-class families from cities to suburbs.

It was here, in the Castle Hill area of the South Bronx, where Jennifer Lopez was born, on July 24, 1970. While the problems of the South Bronx could not be exaggerated, the people who stayed and called the area their home viewed their neighborhoods with a different perspective. While Frank Sinatra may have sung about Manhattan—"If I can make it there/ I'll make it anywhere"—the denizens of South Bronx wear their survival as the true measure of success.

That toughness and the resiliency to overcome harsh odds to succeed are at the very core of who Jennifer Lopez is and has formed her life and career every step of the way. To understand her feistiness and individuality, one first has to understand the environment she grew up in. Although both of her parents had jobs, life was still tough. They lived in a small apartment that she remembers being cold in the winter and hot in the summer. But there was always food on the table.

Like others from the neighborhood, living on the inside looking out from the South Bronx wasn't as scary as it seemed to be for those looking in. "They made this movie called *Fort Apache: The Bronx* and everybody thinks that's what the Bronx is really like, some kind of war zone or something," she once complained to Martyn Palmer of *Total Film*. "It's just like any other inner city. I grew up in what I consider to be a nice neighborhood and for me it was . . . well, it was normal."[2]

And indeed, for whatever mean streets lay outside her front door, the Lopez family home was a safe haven for Jennifer and her two sisters, Lynda and Leslie. Her parents, both Puerto Rican immigrants, were practicing Catholics who made sure their children received a parochial school education. Jennifer's parents took their children to church every Sunday and instilled in them a strong sense of right and wrong. As a youth, Jennifer didn't think much about faith—religion was something she grew up with. But as an adult she would realize how important it was to be spiritual and have a relationship with God.

Her parents also had a decidedly strong work ethic. Her dad, David, was a computer specialist for an insurance company in Manhattan, and her mom, Guadalupe, was employed as a monitor at Holy Family School, which Jennifer attended. Later, Lupe would go to night school to earn her degree and was eventually hired as a kindergarten teacher at the school. Besides being industrious, Lupe Lopez was also strict with her girls, intent on keeping them from falling in with a bad crowd.

As a result, says Jennifer, "I was a good kid. I was always hugging people. I was very close to my grandparents and I listened to my mother and didn't do bad things. I didn't curse and I didn't run around. I was never naughty, but I was a tomboy and very athletic. I'd always be running around and playing sports and stuff. I did gymnastics, competed nationally in track, and was on the school softball team."[3]

Sports were a natural outlet for Jennifer's physical energies but her real passion was performing. Lupe was partial to Broadway musicals and would have her daughters watch them on TV. Jennifer in particular loved watching the performances. Although her parents didn't know it, Jennifer was already fantasizing about being in movies. "But when you're little, you don't really understand what the 'rich and famous' part is all about," Jennifer explains. "It's just a catchphrase that means 'I wanna be doing what they're doing up there.' And ever since I was three that's how I was—I always felt all this drama inside of me."[4]

To her parents, performing was not something that would ever become a career but they encouraged their girls to participate in extracurricular activities in the hopes it would help keep them out of trouble on the street as they got older. So Jennifer was enrolled at *Ballet Hispanico*, a dance school that teaches students both classical ballet and Hispanic dance traditions.

Jennifer remembers going to dance class every weekend at the Kips Bay Boys & Girls Club dance studio in the Bronx. Although she's quick to say her mom was no stage mother, she suspects Lupe may have secretly been a frustrated actress, which is why she encouraged Jennifer and her sisters to participate in the performance arts. As Jennifer got older, she began to pursue dance on her own.

The children are close in age—Lynda is two years younger than middle daughter Jennifer, who herself is just a year younger than Leslie. When at home, the three sisters would act out television series. Their favorite was *Charlie's Angels*. Lynda was always Jaclyn Smith, Leslie was Kate Jackson, and Jennifer always played the blond—first Farrah Fawcett then later Cheryl Ladd. It's ironic that the woman who would later become a role model for ethnic girls everywhere herself had no role model as a child. "There weren't a lot of actresses I could identify with, being Puerto Rican," she points out.[5] One result of having few if any Latin figures to identify with in the media, Jennifer says, is that "if you don't see anybody like you there, it's like, *Well, I guess I don't exist.*"[6]

Which is why, Lupe says, "I made my three daughters watch musical films like *West Side Story.* 'Sit and watch,' I told them, and they did."[7]

Jennifer says she watched *West Side Story* more than a hundred times as a kid. It was her favorite movie and she identified strongly with the characters. "I loved that it was a musical and about Puerto Ricans and that they were living where I lived. I wanted to be Anita because I love to dance and she was Bernardo's girlfriend and he was so hot. But then Maria was the star of the movie. So it was basically like, I gotta be Maria. I think that's the actress in me, wanting to be the center of attention and the star of the show. I just always wanted to achieve and be proud of myself."[8]

Although she gravitated towards musicals because of the dancing involved, music of all kinds influenced Jennifer during her youth. While walking down the streets of her neighborhood Jennifer would hear a symphony of musical styles and genres. "I was in third grade when The Sugarhill Gang's 'Rapper's Delight' changed my life," she says. "But then, when I came home, my mother would be listening to Celia Cruz, Tito Puente, or Diana Ross. That's my background. It's what I call Latin soul."[9] Probably not so coincidentally, Jennifer's sisters would also follow their hearts to careers in music—Lynda is a disc jockey while Leslie works as a music teacher.

Although Jennifer describes herself as a good kid who had caring, attentive parents, she also learned how to handle herself out in the world. No amount of parental love could protect Jennifer and her sisters from the reality of the streets. Life at home was one thing; going to school and growing up among classmates and peers quite another. But at an early age, Jennifer exhibited a tough side.

"She was actually a little devil," says Jennifer's fourth grade teacher Carol McCormack. "That kid didn't take anything from anybody. She was a tough little cookie. I remember I once took her class to meet some actors. She took over the meeting. Jennifer was only eight and there she was, grilling them about what they did and how much they were paid. I just couldn't believe how much nerve she had."[10]

At times, Jennifer seemed to possess two opposite personalities: the same little girl who loved giving out hugs and adored her grandparents was not shy about standing up for herself when the situation called for it, such as the time in fourth grade when she got into a fistfight. "There were these two best friends and I started getting on with one of them," Jennifer recalls. "The other one got jealous, so she told me that the other girl was always talking about me. In the end, I confronted her; she denied it, so I pushed her in the face. We started fighting and I knocked her down. It was pretty ugly, and although I'm not proud of the event, I did win the fight. Nobody ever messed with me after that, and I graduated from school unscathed."[11]

Even so, Jennifer is quick to point out that was then, this is now. "I was nine. I'm not a violent person. Women hitting each other is low class, and it looks ridiculous and stupid. But I can, and would, defend myself if I had to. I'm not going down without a fight, that's for sure. I started that fight in fourth grade, but," she adds, "I've matured since then."[12]

Although she would later become known as one of Hollywood's sultriest sex symbols, as a kid, Jennifer admits her body was slow to develop so she wasn't considered a hottie. However, she stresses she *was* one of the cool kids. Along with her best friend since second grade, Arlene Rodriguez, Jennifer dressed in a style she calls very Bronx, hip-hop, and boyish, in tight jeans and boots. "Then Madonna came along," she says. "I always admired her, liked her music, her sense of style. I like that she changed all the time."[13]

When she was 13, Jennifer had a brush with disaster that could have changed her entire future—a truck carrying compressed gas cylinders hit her mom's car. "The only thing that saved my life was the fact that I was bending down tying my shoes in the front seat, because his headlight flew through the windscreen and ended up in the back of the car. It would have smashed my face in. I don't even remember exactly how my nose got fractured, but that's why it looks like it does. People always tell me I look like I was hit with a hammer, but I like my nose. In profile it's good, but if you look straight at me or touch it, you can see the flatness."[14]

Her broken nose and the character it gave her face ultimately only added to her blossoming looks as a Latin beauty. Unlike some girls who prefer to play the field, Jennifer preferred to have a steady boyfriend, although she didn't date much as a kid. Her first crush happened in the third grade with a boy named Charles who had blue eyes and black hair. "He was so cute. I never kissed him because I was only ten years old. He'd come over to my house every day and my mom would give us sandwiches and milk. I dreamt of marrying him. I saw him years later when he'd grown up, and let's put it this way—he peaked early," she laughs.[15]

When she was eleven, Jennifer's body began to develop the curves for which it would later become famous. Lupe constantly worried about

Jennifer being so sexy, fearful her daughter would end up pregnant. "The taste in my neighborhood was for voluptuous women," Jennifer explains. "I knew guys liked me. In the third, fourth grade, there were girls who already . . . were always kissing in the school closet. Not me. I was more of a late bloomer."[16]

In the tenth grade Jennifer started dating her first real boyfriend, David Cruz. "He made me feel like a hot babe," Jennifer says, noting, "We started dating when I was 15 and dated only each other for nine years. We were very careful. I'm not saying we weren't having sex, because we were," she admits.[17] But unlike her daydreams about Charles, by this time Jennifer was far more interested in pursuing a career than settling down. She was also developing her own sense of style, putting together outfits based on pictures she saw in fashion magazines.

"Everybody would look at me, like I was a nerd—*What is she doing? What is she wearing?*—because people didn't do that in my neighborhood; people didn't work out or take care of their bodies. If people see you striving for things, it threatens them."[18] Cruz understood Jennifer had bigger plans than most people but sometimes others would accuse Jennifer of being too ambitious. She would simply shrug and let the implied insult roll over her.

Although in her heart Jennifer believed she could achieve whatever she put her mind to, she also had a practical side and for a while, intended to get her license to be a hair-stylist. Her first job was in a salon sweeping up the hair from the floor. At home she would practice her technique on her patient sisters. The results were less than stellar, Jennifer admits, because she had no idea what she was doing.

In high school, Jennifer was a good student earning high grades, and a natural athlete. She played softball, was a skilled gymnast, and competed in track. She also participated in all the plays and continued taking dance classes. Even though she never hid her passion for performing, Jennifer's parents still assumed she would pursue a more practical and stable career. "Where I come from, you got a job as a bank teller and got married and being driven didn't mean wanting to be a star. It meant being a lawyer instead of a secretary." Although being an attorney "was aiming really high where I came from," says Jennifer, "it was an attainable goal."[19]

And for a while, she tried to juggle her parents' expectations with her personal aspirations but soon realized she had to live her own life, whatever the consequences. That said, it was still hard to tell her parents she was dropping out of Baruch College in New York City after only one semester to devote herself to being a dancer. Their response was understandably less than enthusiastic.

"It was a fight from the beginning," admits Jennifer. "When I told my parents I wasn't going to college and law school, they thought it was really stupid to go off and try to be a movie star. No Latinas did that. It was just this stupid, foolish, crapshoot idea to my parents and to everybody who knew me."[20]

Jennifer wasn't willing to let the lack of support from family or friends deter her ambition but she was still faced with a problem: She knew she wanted to perform as a career but she didn't know how to go about it. So she would take the No. 6 subway train into Manhattan—which years later would be the inspiration for the title of her first album, *On the 6*—to dance studios, including the Manhattan Dance Studio on West 19th Street in Greenwich Village, where she studied ballet and jazz. She also went on any audition she could find. Jennifer says that was a particularly happy time for her. "To me, the struggle has always been the fun part."[21] Soon the 19 year old found herself living the exciting but always tenuous life of a *gypsy*, the Broadway term for a professional dancer.

Devoting herself completely to dance often meant scraping by on little money. "There were times when I was really down to my last dollar," she recalls. "And then my last 50 cents . . . and then my last quarter. I'd dance in a piece-of-garbage rap or pop video for 50 bucks and make the money last a whole month."[22]

A turning point for Jennifer came after M. C. Hammer came out with his mega-hit "You Can't Touch This." "All the auditions started becoming hip-hop auditions," remembers Jennifer. "I was good at it, and they were like, 'Ooh, a light-skinned girl who can do that. Great, let's hire her!'"[23]

In 1988 Jennifer spent five months touring Europe with the *Golden Musicals of Broadway* review. During that trip, Jennifer became depressed when she was the only dancer not given a solo. She called her mom in tears but Lupe opted for tough love, telling Jennifer she *never* wanted to catch her crying. Jennifer later said it was the best advice anyone ever gave her because it just made her try harder and become that much more committed—nobody was asking Jennifer to be a performer. If she wanted it, she'd have to go out and get it—and she did. Jennifer later appeared in the chorus of Hinton Battle's musical, *Synchronicity*, in Japan. She also performed in regional productions of *Oklahoma* and *Jesus Christ Superstar*.

But she learned that she wasn't cut out for every performing role. Jennifer recalls her first commercial audition in 1989, for a promotional ad for the Olympics, during which the director asked her if she knew how to use a trampoline. Without hesitation, she assured him *of course* she did . . . even though she had never been on one before in her life. Still, confidence in her physical and athletic abilities gave Jennifer the necessary belief that she *could* do whatever they asked of her. And without hesitation, the director hired her.

As it turned out, the commercial was never broadcast and perhaps for the better because, according to Jennifer, she was terrible in it. The problem, she would later come to believe, is that commercial work by its very nature is just too superficial for her. So she stopped going on those auditions. When it came to being a talking head or mouthpiece for an advertiser, Jennifer quickly realized she simply wasn't convincing. However, for whatever financial resources she may have lost by turning her back on television commercials, Jennifer would gain in focus and rededicated drive. She also had another invaluable quality—emotional thick skin. "My older sister and I both started out in musical theater," Jennifer notes. "She has a great voice and she had more of a chance of making it than I did. But she couldn't take the rejection."[24] But Jennifer could. "If you're gonna make it in this business, you need the kind of personality that, you have to do it or die, there's no alternative."[25]

So when Jennifer came to Los Angeles to test her performing wings on *In Living Color,* she approached it as a matter of creative life and death.

NOTES

1. Jim Fricke and Charlie Ahearn (Editors). *Yes Yes Y'All: The Experience Music Project Oral History of Hip-Hop's First Decade.* Cambridge, MA: Da Capo Press, 2002.

2. Martyn Palmer. "Sex and the Sisco Kid." *The Mirror,* November 27, 1998. http://www.highbeam.com/doc/1G1–60628260.html.

3. Anthony Noguera. *FHM,* December 1998. http://www.beyond-beautiful. org/topic/412/t/FHM-December-1998.html.

4. Brantley Bardin. "Woman Of The Year: Jennifer Lopez." *Details,* December 1998. http://members.aol.com/dafreshprinz/jenniferlopez/details1298.htm.

5. Julian Ives. *Mr. Showbiz,* 1997. http://www.lovelylopez.net/mrshowbiz interview.php.

6. Virginia Rohan. "The Spirit of Selena." *The Record* (Bergen County, NY). March 20, 1997, pp. y01. http://www.highbeam.com/doc/1P1–22391245.html.

7. Dennis Duggan. "A Rising Latina Star Wows Them in Bronx." *Newsday,* March 20, 1997, A04.

8. Brantley Bardin. "Woman Of The Year: Jennifer Lopez." *Details,* December 1998. http://members.aol.com/dafreshprinz/jenniferlopez/details1298.htm.

9. Michael A. Gonzales. "Jennifer's Many Phases." *Latina,* March 1999. http://www.toppics4u.com/jennifer_lopez/i1.html.

10. David Gardner. "Jennifer Lopez: La Guitara Was So Darned Hot She'd Burn You." *Sunday Mirror,* June 17, 2001. http://www.highbeam.com/doc/1P2–6053243.html.

11. Anthony Noguera. *FHM*, December 1998. http://www.beyond-beautiful.org/topic/412/t/FHM-December-1998.html.

12. Michael A. Gonzales. "Jennifer's Many Phases." *Latina*, March 1999. http://www.toppics4u.com/jennifer_lopez/i1.html.

13. Anthony Noguera. *FHM*, December 1998. http://www.beyond-beautiful.org/topic/412/t/FHM-December-1998.html.

14. Ibid.

15. Ibid.

16. Douglas Thompson. "Jennifer Lopez: The ego has landed." *Sunday Mirror*, November 15, 1998. http://www.highbeam.com/doc/1G1–60646155.html.

17. Ibid.

18. Stephen Rebello. "The Wow." *Movieline*, February 1998. http://members.aol.com/dafreshprinz/jenniferlopez/movieline0298.htm.

19. Bob Strauss. "Blood and Guts." *Chicago Sun-Times*, February 16, 1997. http://www.highbeam.com/doc/1P2–4374767.html.

20. Ibid.

21. Bob Morris. "Could This be Love?" *Talk Magazine*, March 2000. http://beautiful962.yuku.com/topic/4034/t/Talk-Magazine-March-2000.html.

22. Michael A. Gonzales. "Jennifer's Many Phases." *Latina*, March 1999. http://www.toppics4u.com/jennifer_lopez/i1.html.

23. David Handleman. "A Diva Is Born." *Mirabella*, August 1998. http://members.aol.com/dafreshprinz/jenniferlopez/mirabella0898.htm.

24. Ibid.

25. Ibid.

Chapter 2

GOTTA DANCE

Dancing has always been Jennifer Lopez's first love and initially her professional goals were solely dance related. She admits that for a long time, she didn't understand why a dancer would want to become an actor. Eventually, though, she would. Dance is a very specific form of physical expression, but for someone who yearns to express themselves more broadly, acting and singing offer a more internal creative outlet.

In 1990, FOX put out a national casting call for dancers to work on *In Living Color*, a new comedy sketch show the network was developing with actor–comedian Keenan Ivory Wayans. Along with thousands of other hopefuls, Jennifer tried out for the job, going through a series of auditions, each one more nerve-wracking than the previous one because with each callback, the chances of getting the job increased significantly. When the final cut was made, Jennifer, along with Lisa Marie Todd and Michelle Whitney-Morrison were hired as the "Fly Girls" who would appear on the series and be choreographed by Rosie Perez, an actress-dancer who was nominated for a Best Supporting Actress Oscar in 1993 for *Fearless*. In addition to being a hit show for FOX, the series succeeded in breaking color barriers.

With some notable exceptions, since the early 1980s, broadcast television programming has mostly reflected a white, middle-class suburban sensibility, particularly in its comedy shows. What *In Living Color* did was bring the urban hip-hop culture into the American heartland, without apology and often without any sense of political correctness. It was an instant hit.

Hip-hop culture, and the music genre it spawned, originated in New York City in the 1970s among the Latino and African American neighborhoods. The main elements to hip-hop culture were tagging, or graffiti art; deejaying; emceeing, or rapping; and breakdancing. Hip-hop devotees also developed their own style of dress, their own slang, and, ultimately, their own music genre.

The first hip-hop music happened when club DJs started isolating the percussion beat from disco or funk songs to play as dance music. The MC was there to introduce the DJ or the music and to generate excitement among the crowd. The MC would talk between songs, which evolved into rapping. By 1979 hip-hop music was being accepted by mainstream radio and consumers in the United States and abroad.

In Living Color held very little sacred and stretched the limits of network censors by introducing characters such as Handi-Man, a superhero with cerebral palsy; the Home Boys, a pair of con artists who chanted for "mo' money"; *Hey Mon*, the adventures of a hard-working West Indian family; and Blaine and Antoine, a flamboyantly gay version of Siskel and Ebert. Reveling in their weekly madness was a crop of then-newcomers, including several of Keenan's own brothers and sisters, many of whom would go on to individual success. Rosie Perez would segue from choreography to being an Oscar-nominated actress; David Alan Grier would star in a comedy series of his own and return to his theater roots by starring in a Broadway revival of *A Funny Thing Happened on the Way to the Forum*; Damon Wayans would find success as a television writer; and James Carrey would go on to become known as Jim Carrey, one of the movie world's $20-million-dollar men.

Because of the show's admittedly sexually charged content and innuendo, from the outside looking in, it might have seemed that being one of the voluptuous Fly Girls might have meant constantly fielding suggestive comments or more from the hormonally charged male cast members. But Jennifer says the filming schedule prevented too much close contact. "We were separated. We rehearsed in different rooms, and we only taped on one day when they weren't there. But we knew them and they were great to us. It was a good show . . . hip and cool."[1]

Although *In Living Color* only averaged an overall 1 to 1.5 Nielsen rating, it reached the young 18- to-34-year-old demographic FOX—and its advertisers—coveted. So it was poised for a long run until egos and politics brought it to a premature end. During midseason of the 1992–93 season, Fox informed Keenan that they were going to air reruns of the show in place of another series that had been canceled. Wayans vehemently objected, claiming the extra exposure would hurt the syndication value of the show. When the network went ahead with their plan to broadcast the show twice a week, Wayans, along with all his brothers and sisters, abruptly quit while it was still in production. Although the show finished out the third season and would last another year, the defections proved fatal and *In Living Color* aired its last original episode in August 1994.

While the demise of the series was a bitter ending for the Wayans clan, for Jennifer the series had always been one door to walk through before opening another. Although she was strictly a background player and only those viewers with a yen for reading credits would have known her name, her years on *In Living Color* were an invaluable learning experience, not to mention a steady paycheck. So when she wasn't working on the series, she devoted herself to taking acting lessons to prepare herself for the speaking roles she was confident would follow. If there was a downside to working on the show, it meant Jennifer had to relocate to Los Angeles during the filming. Leaving her adored—and adoring—family behind left Jennifer homesick, and there was a time when she contemplated leaving. But Keenan advised her to stick it out, telling her she would have more money and more experience if she stayed.

Staying also resulted in Jennifer finding her first talent manager. Eric Gold was a co-producer on the series, and her furious ambition and dedication convinced him Jennifer was a star just waiting to happen. "There was just an unshakable confidence about Jennifer," says Gold, who signed Jennifer as a client in 1992. "No doubt, no fear. The girl just had it."[2] He had almost as much confidence in Jennifer's future as she did and eventually he would leave producing to concentrate on promoting Jennifer's career.

One of his first observations as her manager was to tell Jennifer she needed to lose weight if she wanted to act. Gold recalls that "the very next day she had a trainer and was out jogging."[3] For Gold, *In Living Color* would prove to be a double goldmine—Eric also signed Jim Carrey as a client and turned him into one of the highest-paid actors in film.

However, Jennifer was more concerned with creating opportunities for herself than with making money, and her work ethic paid off almost immediately. In 1993 Jennifer found work on some high-profile music videos, such as Janet Jackson's "That's The Way Love Goes." That same year she also appeared in the otherwise forgettable television movie *Nurses on the Line: The Crash of Flight 7*, starring Lyndsay Wagner as one of a group of student nurses whose plane crashes in the Mexican jungle. And before *In Living Color* had wrapped production, Jennifer was offered another series job.

As often happens in Hollywood, jobs come through people you know. In this case, a member of the show's production team was married to a producer-writer who was working on a new drama for FOX called *South Central* and suggested to her husband that he audition Jennifer for a part. He did and she was eventually hired as the recurring character of Lucy, who works at a local co-op. The story revolved around a divorcee, played by Tina Lifford, who loses her job and goes to work as an assistant manager of a food co-op. *South Central* was one of the first serious attempts by a network to launch a black "dramedy."

As such, prior to its debut in 1994, the series generated a lot of buzz. But by the time the show aired, buzz had turned to scrutiny. Setting a series in L.A.'s notorious South Central district was risky enough but playing it occasionally for laughs seemed creative suicide. Critics, however, were willing to give the show some breathing room. *Newsday* noted, "Lifford's character has just lost her job; she fears she's losing her son to the streets; she's already lost too many of the important men in her life, and she's wondering whether her sanity is the next element out the door . . . The folks here know laughing about it ain't gonna make it better. But they laugh anyway. And they ask us to, too."[4]

While some may have thought it was in poor taste to find humor in despair and social inequity, creator Ralph Farquhar, who himself is a product of Chicago's equally notorious South Side, disagreed. "What I think we've managed to accomplish is that drama and comedy occupy the same space. One doesn't end where the other begins. There's comedy within the dramatic moments, or drama within the comedy."[5]

In one episode, the characters humorously debate the merits of being called African-American as opposed to black. "We're going to touch all sides," Farquhar promised in the weeks leading up to the show's first broadcast. "You know, TV tends to be stacked. We're going to dare to be politically incorrect, if that suits the characters' points of view. The show takes a basically neutral position."[6]

When *South Central* premiered in April 1994, many viewers found it neither funny nor easy to follow. One of Farquhar's other ideas was to present a show that plays out like a true slice of life, meaning that characters suddenly appear without introduction and the story lines are presented in a non-linear manner. "There's enough TV that tells you everything three times, just so you can get it," Farquhar complained. "On this, we were more concerned with the emotion of it. That leaves a lot sometimes to one's imagination. But there's a lot of debate that comes as a result of viewing TV this way."[7]

For all the good intentions of FOX and Farquhar, *South Central* never found an audience. For as much as networks had been criticized for not having multicultural programming on the air, the series came under fire almost immediately from an unexpected constituency—the very black community the producers sought to represent, who accused the show of promoting racial stereotypes.

Actress Marianne Aalda-Gedeon complained, "Basically they're saying that a show about an unemployed woman who's been deserted by her husband to raise three foul-mouthed, disrespectful, beeper-carrying, front-yard-urinating kids is as good as it gets? And I'm supposed to like it? I don't think so. I mean, this mother, with the way she is, would not have raised children who acted like this. I know this because I don't allow that behavior in my home, and neither does any other African-American mother I know."[8]

Even Bill Cosby got into the fray. Speaking during his induction into the Academy of Television Arts and Sciences Hall of Fame, he lost his funnyman persona to chastise the television industry. "Stop this horrible massacre of images that are being put on the screen now," he scolded. "I'm begging you, because it isn't us."[9]

For Jennifer, the brouhaha was secondary to the excitement of having her first real acting job. She was glad the show generated interest of any kind and hoped it would last long enough to give her some much needed on-the-job experience. Plus, for the second time during her still-fledgling career, Jennifer was associated with projects that pushed both the creative envelope of Hollywood's entertainment community and the social buttons of the audience. Being involved in something new and pioneering appealed to her personal and professional sensibilities, and she was proud to have the shows on her résumé.

While *South Central* may have broken new ground, the series was on shaky terrain from the start. The show was canceled and its last episode aired in August 1994. When FOX subsequently also canceled *Roc* and *Sinbad*, two other programs with predominantly minority casts, the number of shows with black or Latino leads were practically nonexistent on primetime broadcast TV. The reaction was passionate.

Roc star Charles Dutton angrily sounded off during an interview, calling his show a victim of a new racial segregation that says, "No blacks, Latins or dogs need apply after 9 p.m.,"[10] the time network programmers generally broadcast their serious dramas. Critics were equally concerned at the trend. In a column for the *St. Louis Post-Dispatch*, Clarence Page wondered, "Imagine, for a moment, the public outcry if the networks were to announce that, in the new fall season, *Blossom* and *Married . . . with Children* would be the only prime-time network television programs that would portray the lives of white people in America. Right. It couldn't happen. Audiences would not tolerate such a narrow portrayal of white people. The public would demand more diversity—more dramas, more docu-dramas, more action, more soaps, more stories of love, more stories of hate, more triumph, more tragedy, more of a reflection of real life as we know it."[11]

Page singled out *Blossom* and *Married . . . With Children* because those sitcoms had the distinction of being the only two predominantly white programs that, according to a survey of black vs. white viewing habits, were in the Top 10 among black viewers. "In other words," Page concluded, "blacks, like whites, love to see whites cavort in situation comedies. That's OK. The marketplace works best when it offers choices. Comedy thrives on stereotypes. But life thrives on variety. In the absence of any other images, stereotypes become a form of real-life tragedy."[12]

Moreover, with so few roles for minorities available in the best of times, the cancellation of those three shows put a lot of talented minority actors out of work, many of whom would struggle to find another job. However, that was not the case with Jennifer Lopez. Even though *South Central* went off the air after only a couple of months, it was a long enough run to give Jennifer enough exposure to catch the eyes of Hollywood executives who were looking to add minorities of any shade to their casts to ward off the increasing criticism by coalitions and critics alike.

For Jennifer, it would truly be a case of being in the right profession at just the right time in Hollywood history. Like astrological bodies moving into alignment, her boundless energy and dedication were propelling her forward within an entertainment community more willing than ever to consider the possibilities that leading ladies didn't all necessarily have to be blue-eyed blonds from Nebraska; that names with an ethnic ring weren't box office or ratings poison; that modern-day sex symbols didn't always have to look as if they were suffering from some eating disorder.

Anyone insisting on clinging to the stereotypical Hollywood projection of beauty would one day get burned in Jennifer Lopez's star vapor trail as she passed them by. But first, she was willing to keep paying her dues.

Jennifer's next series, *Second Chances*, was going to give her the chance to show off some dramatic acting chops. The series was set in the fictional seaside town of Santa Rita, California, and was categorized as a serial drama-romantic mystery. It starred Connie Sellecca, best known for two earlier series: *The Greatest American Hero* and *Hotel*. The ensemble drama also starred Justin Lazard as Jennifer's love interest.

The plot of the show revolved around three women. Sellecca played Dianne Benedict, a public defender who hopes to be elected a judge. She is also a single mother of an eight-year-old son. Megam Porter Follows co-starred as Benedict's sister Kate, who has a penchant for picking the wrong man. Jennifer's character, Melinda Lopez, is a waitress who ends up marrying a law student from a wealthy family whose parents just happen to be racists, making for a short-lived honeymoon. For the first time, Jennifer was in a legitimate co-starring role.

Many critics embraced the show. "You've got to like a show like this spunky new serial that hits the ground sprinting," wrote David Hiltbrand in *People*. "These are clearly not women to be trifled with . . . The show's scope is a little narrow. But it is impertinent and eventful."[13]

Unfortunately, though, *Second Chances* aired opposite the extremely popular *L.A. Law*. So even before the series went on the air, the producers knew they were facing a big challenge to find an audience. So they turned to technology and became one of the first shows to use the Internet to further its cause. Beginning the night of its premiere on December 2, 1993, *Second Chances* established its own chat rooms where fans could discuss the show. The potential power of this then-new communication medium wasn't lost on some future-thinking network executives who recognized that chat rooms were a view into fan interest to which the usual Nielsen TV rating system was blind and deaf. And monitoring chat rooms became a regular part of their day.

Being the third lead on a primetime series was getting Jennifer more attention than she'd ever experienced—and her first taste of celebrity. In December 1993, she was asked to co-host a CBS New Year's Day special called *Coming up Roses* that aired prior to the telecast of the Tournament of Roses Parade. Sitting behind a rose-bedecked podium under a warm December California sun must have seemed like a very long way from the Bronx for Jennifer.

Thanks in large part to their vocal fans, *Second Chances* stayed on the air despite low ratings. But what the cast and network didn't know was that series star Connie Sellecca was hiding a very big secret. She and her husband, *Entertainment Tonight* anchor John Tesh, were expecting a baby. Her reason for not immediately telling the producers was more superstition than deception—Sellecca had suffered a miscarriage in August 1993 and wanted to wait until her first trimester had passed before announcing her pregnancy. However, when pressed, she also admitted she was worried that the network might be less apt to pick the show up for the next season if they knew she was pregnant.

However, keeping her condition under wraps proved difficult. "I was very sick, which made working that much more difficult," she revealed in a *Good Housekeeping* interview. "I tried to run to my dressing room before I threw up."[14] But it's almost impossible to keep a secret on a film or television set and someone who overheard Sellecca gagging in the bathroom reported it to the producers. However, aware and leery that a pregnancy might impact negatively on their renewal decision, the producers kept Connie's condition to themselves. Once CBS gave them the green light for more episodes Sellecca and Tesh made the announcement. Suddenly, Jennifer was on the brink of becoming a genuine television star.

Then at 4:31 A.M. on January 17, 1994, everything changed.

The Northridge earthquake hit with such sudden force, brick fireplace chimneys snapped off houses and were smashed into so much pottery. End tables flew across bedrooms and splintered against walls. People were jerked out of sound sleeps to find themselves on the floor, trying to hold on until the shaking stopped. While not the dreaded Big One geologists keep predicting, it was obvious to longtime residents that this had been a bad one. The worst hit areas were in the San Fernando Valley. Certain areas experienced liquefaction, meaning the soil beneath the houses literally dissolved under the stress. The floor of the valley moved several inches north and the nearby mountains grew an astonishing 15 inches in height as a result of the earth's movement. It was an awe-inspiring display of nature that affected everyone in its path.

Jennifer came through unscathed but the production facility where *Second Chances* filmed—located in Valencia, about 20 minutes north of the valley—suffered extensive damage. The earthquake forced CBS to juggle its schedule, and they took *Second Chances* off the air for six weeks, although the producers and CBS fully expected the series to go forward. But the damage proved too much to overcome.

"We thought we'd come up running, but at first we couldn't even get into our production facilities, and when we did, we found that water from burst overhead pipes had ruined everything," executive producer Bernard Lechowick said.[15] The 22-episode order was cut to 9, with the final installment airing late one night after David Letterman. Despite everyone's desire to keep the show going and to film the full 22 episodes, the production was officially canceled.

Although bitterly disappointed, Jennifer realized you couldn't fight an act of God. Plus, she had reason to be optimistic; the series had given her the chance to show she was more than just a dancer. It also had given her an important foot in the door; she was one of the very few Latin actresses to be seen on prime time and she looked every bit at home in that setting. Certainly CBS, as well as Bernard Lechowick and his producing partner—and wife—Lynn Marie Latham, recognized a special quality in Jennifer, and it wasn't long before Jennifer was back in business with them.

Because of the circumstances surrounding the abbreviated production of *Second Chances*, CBS asked Latham and Lechowick to develop another series for the network. The idea they came up with centered around the hotel restaurant business. "We're always doing research," says Lechowick, "and we'd been collecting information about the hotel-restaurant business for a full three years, interviewing any employee who'd talk to us when we were on vacation with the kids or just out to dinner."[16]

One thing that jumped out at them was that people who worked in those jobs liked it. So the series would revolve around the family-run hotel's wealthy owners and their staff. The network gave the series, called *Hotel Malibu*, an initial six-episode order. Among the characters who would inhabit the hotel's world were two holdovers from *Second Chances*— Jennifer's Melinda Lopez character, as well as her father Sal, played by Pepe Serna. The network had agreed with Latham and Lechowick that television didn't have enough strong, Hispanic families.

Hotel Malibu starred Joanna Cassidy as the widowed, still-grieving owner of the hotel who finds a second chance at love with her old high school sweetheart, Sal Lopez. Although there were some kind reviews, *Hotel Malibu* found little favor with audiences and even less with critics. CBS aired the six episodes of *Hotel Malibu* between August 4 and September 8, with no intention of renewing the summer series for its regular season schedule.

Despite the failure of either *Second Chances* or *Hotel Malibu* to become a hit, CBS was anxious to continue their association with Jennifer and offered her a financially attractive development deal of her own. It was an opportunity many actors would jump at, especially one as young as Jennifer. But she knew it wasn't the direction she wanted her career to go and turned down the deal.

Jennifer had learned a lot during her time working on television, but she had her sights set on a bigger goal—Jennifer was ready to make her dream of being a movie star come true.

NOTES

1. Neal Justin. "The wonderful world of 'Color.'" *Minneapolis Star Tribune*, August 26, 1997, p. 01E.

2. David Handleman. "A Diva is Born." *Mirabella*, July/August 1998.

3. Bob Morris. "Could This be Love?" *Talk Magazine*, March 2000. http://beautiful962.yuku.com/topic/4034/t/Talk-Magazine-March-2000.html.

4. "Glued to the Tube: Comedy, Drama—Get It?" *Newsday*, April 5, 1994, p. B57.

5. Ray Richmond. "'South Central' Criticized As Depicting Stereotypes." *Los Angeles Daily News*, *St. Louis Post-Dispatch*, May 5, 1994, p. 06G.

6. Ibid.

7. Clarence Page. "Networks Tune Out Black Americans." *St. Louis Post-Dispatch*, June 9, 1994, p. 07B.

8. Ray Richmond. "'South Central' Criticized As Depicting Stereotypes." *Los Angeles Daily News, St. Louis Post-Dispatch*, May 5, 1994, p. 06G.

9. Isabel Wilkerson. "Television; Black Life on TV: Realism or Stereotypes?" *New York Times*, August 15, 1993. Available at http://query.nytimes.com/gst/full page.html?res=9F0CE7DD1339F936A2575BC0A965958260&sec=&spon=& pagewanted=2.

10. Clarence Page. "Networks Tune Out Black Americans." *St. Louis Post-Dispatch*, June 9, 1994, p. 07B.

11. Ibid.

12. Ibid.

13. David Hiltbrand. "Picks & Pans." *People*, December 20, 1993, p. 13.

14. Bob Thomas. "Connie & John: Lessons in Love." *Good Housekeeping*, March 1, 1994, p. 126(3).

15. Gail Pennington. "'Hotel Malibu' Checks In." *St. Louis Post-Dispatch*, August 4, 1994, p. 01G.

16. Television Critics Association Press tour attended by author. Held July 1994 at the Ritz-Carlton in Pasadena California.

Chapter 3

ACTING BECKONS

While CBS executives were genuinely impressed with Jennifer's charisma and screen appeal, the development deal they offered wasn't without political ulterior motives. In September 1994, the television networks were placed on notice after a study commissioned by a Latino advocacy group presented findings that showed Hispanics were less visible on prime time in the mid-1990s than they had been in the 1950s, when Desi Arnaz, Jr., starred on *I Love Lucy*, and *Zorro* was one of the most popular adventure series. Despite making up almost 10 percent of the American population, Hispanics comprised only 1 percent of all characters portrayed during the 1992–93 season. By contrast, African Americans, who account for 12 percent of the general population, were seen in 17 percent of the available roles television had to offer.[1]

"Hispanics remain virtually invisible on prime-time entertainment. The proportion of Latino characters has been declining since the 1950s," said S. Robert Lichter who co-authored the 55-page report *Distorted Reality: Hispanic Characters in TV Entertainment*. More disturbing were the statistics that suggested when Latinos did appear as characters, it was primarily in an unsavory light, such as criminals or drug addicts. Of the Hispanic characters who were seen, 16 percent committed crimes, compared with only 4 percent for both blacks and whites. Shows like FOX's *Cops* "basically . . . consist of whites arresting minorities."[2]

"This is systematic slander," said Raul Yzaguirre, president of the National Council of La Raza, a Hispanic civil rights group that commissioned the report. "We're very concerned about the negative portrayal of Hispanics." For Yzaguirre, it wasn't a matter of cultural or ethnic pride at issue nor, he said, was it about "one group trying to get more attention. It's about defining America. Television is robbing an entire society of reality. We're putting the networks on notice."[3]

Gregory Freeman of the *St. Louis Dispatch* thoughtfully noted that "for whatever reason, Hollywood has been slow to react to the increasing diversity in America. For blacks, that's often meant silly programming designed to appeal to the lowest common denominator. But for Hispanics, it has often meant no portrayals at all or portrayals as criminals."[4]

Freeman went on to point out that "the increase of blacks on television began during the peak of the civil rights movement, during the 1960s," and that in order for change to occur, you've got to make some noise. He ended his column by noting, "It's too bad that anyone should have to say anything at all about Hollywood's portrayals. But the entertainment industry is one that traditionally has been built on stereotypes. The only way to battle those stereotypes is to stand up and be counted."[5]

For Jennifer, the best way to be counted was through her work and her refusal to let her ethnic heritage stand in the way. She was proud of her Puerto Rican background but at the same time felt she was just as American as any other girl next door. However, it would take a firmly Hispanic role in 1995's *My Family (Mi Familia)* to break her out and turn casting agents color blind when it came to hiring her.

The director who cast her was Gregory Nava. He first got the attention of the Hollywood film industry with his 1983 independent film *El Norte*, which presented Latinos as three-dimensional characters. The movie followed a Guatemalan brother and sister who flee their troubled homeland and make their way to *El Norte*—the United States. The film received rave critical reviews and Nava's script, which he co-wrote with Anna Thomas, was nominated for an Academy Award. It made him not only the best-known Latino director but the *only* known Latino director in Hollywood.

In *My Family (Mi Familia)*, Nava and Thomas returned to themes similar to those explored in *El Norte*. This time the story focused on three generations of Latinos in the 1920s, 1950s, and 1980s who try to find their place in America's complicated melting pot culture. The family history is recounted by the eldest living son Paco (Edward James Olmos), who narrates the film.

Jennifer's storyline is set in the 1920s segment. It begins with a teenaged Jose Sanchez leaving his Mexican village and traveling to Los Angeles to find his only living relative. With no means and no money, Jose has to walk to Los Angeles and once there, finds his relative, who is known as El California because he is a direct descendant from the original California settlers. Jose moves in and sets out to make a life in his new home. Jose finds a job as a gardener in Beverly Hills, where he meets the beautiful Maria, played in her younger years by Jennifer, who works as a house-keeper at one of the city's palatial homes. Jose and Maria find love and get married with high hopes for their future. When the Great Depression hits, Maria and Jose still manage to make do. But their peaceful world is destroyed when Maria is picked up during an immigration sweep, loaded into a railroad boxcar, and deported to Mexico—even though she is a U.S. citizen. More than just a dramatic device, the scene represents an unthinkable but historically accurate and then-common practice of the Immigration Service during that period of time.

Unaware what has happened, Jose is frantic but knows he has to keep it together for his children. Back in Mexico, Maria is stranded with no money and no way to contact Jose, but she is determined to keep her fam-ily together. After she gives birth to her son Chucho, she sets off for Los Angeles. It takes her almost a year, but Maria finally rejoins Jose and the family is reunited.

Although Jennifer was familiar with the life of Puerto Rican immi-grants having grown up in the Bronx, playing Maria gave her a new un-derstanding of Mexican immigrants. The depth and texture of the film came from Nava's own personal experience. "Although I was born and raised in San Diego—I'm a third generation native Californian—some of my immediate relatives, who live just a few miles from the house I was raised in, are Mexican. So I've always been raised in that border world, with that tremendous clash between the cultures."[6]

Even though Nava was well aware the subject of Latin underrepresenta-tion in the media was a hot button issue, he refused to pitch his film as a political statement. "I see My Family as a film to entertain people, not to teach them. I think that films need to entertain us, and I mean entertain in the broadest sense of the word, which is partially to enlighten us about who we are. So it is designed to be inspirational to people but it's also designed to give people a good night out at the movies. It makes you laugh, it makes you cry, it makes you feel dignity or pride if you're a Chicano, to be Chicano."[7]

That said, Nava believed the audience was ready for views from other shades of American culture. "I hope we will be able to see more images up on the screen that are . . . not stereotypic but that are positive. Images that allow us to retain our culture—one which is thousands of years old, with very deep roots—and which has something very beautiful to contribute to the nation."[8]

For Jennifer, making this movie was a career-affirming experience. While she would always appreciate her time on the television series, she knew instinctively, this was her medium. Movies would be the place where she would make her ultimate mark as an actress, and not just a Latin actress.

"My managers and agents and I realized that I'm not white," she once said, "so I've always wanted to show that I could play any kind of character; not only a range of emotions, but also race-wise."[9]

Jennifer was proud to have been associated with Mi Familia. And even before its release, her performance was generating enough buzz that it carried her directly into another film that would start Jennifer on the road to being a sex symbol.

Moreover, going from the artistically serious My Family/Mi Familia to co-starring opposite Woody Harrelson and Wesley Snipes in 1995's Money Train gave Jennifer a firsthand look at the extremes in Hollywood moviemaking. While everyone on My Family shared a certain sense of purpose because of the subject matter and because of their bond as Latino actors, Money Train's sole reason to be was to make money without having to think too much about things like plot and structure.

For Harrelson, Money Train was coming along two years after the end of Cheers, the television series that had been his big career break. In the film, which was written with four intersecting plot lines, Harrelson and Snipes play Charlie and John. When Charlie was little, John's family took him in as a foster child and later adopted him. As a result, Charlie is always trying to stay in touch with his black "heritage," much to John's constant bemusement.

Both brothers work as New York Metropolitan Transit Authority Police officers and one storyline concerns the brothers' rivalry over fellow officer Grace Santiago, played by Jennifer. "She's a very attractive police officer who is also somewhat provocative to both brothers," Snipes explained while promoting the film. "Charlie gets the hots for her, but he basically doesn't have a snowball's chance in hell of getting her. She, of course, chooses me, which is the likely scenario."[10]

Although the movie was mostly shot on location in New York, the stunt sequences were filmed at a working, 15-car, half-mile-long subway set built on an old Southern Pacific railway track near Chinatown in Los Angeles. The set, which cost over $4 million to build, was so realistic, Jennifer says, "It even had that yellowness that creeps halfway up the tiles that used to be white. It was exactly like a real subway, except it didn't smell. It was so authentic, I felt like I could take the train home."[11]

For Jennifer, who beat out over one hundred other actresses for the role, getting to film a movie in New York was a wonderful homecoming. Money Train's director, Joseph Ruben, was effusive in his praise of Jennifer.

"Grace had to be first of all believable . . . You had to believe that she grew up in New York City, that she was a tough, strong New York Cop. On top of that, she had to be one hell of an actor with humor and a lot of spirit. And Jennifer fit the bill. She's the real thing."[12]

Ruben and the others discovered that Jennifer didn't just play tough; she *was* tough. When she discovered that her character would be carrying a .38 mm revolver while John and Charlie were issued 9 mms, she demanded equal firearm rights. "A .38 is such a girl gun," Jennifer said, noting that she once dated a policeman. "I'm not going to carry some sissy revolver."[13] Duly chastened, the production prop man rectified the inequity and Jennifer got her big gun.

She may be a sissy but a peek into her purse would reveal she *was* the typical girl next door. When asked once what she carried in her bag, Jennifer rattled off brands of lipstick, lip gloss, face power, make-up foundation, nail polish, mascara, lip liner, eye liner "and Origins mint facial wash. I always take my cellular phone and pager, and workout gloves for the gym. Inevitably, there are stray dollar bills floating around the bottom and tampons."[14]

Jennifer insisted that she wasn't married to any one particular look or fashion. "Going-out-at-night makeup depends on what I'm wearing, or my mood, or how I've done my hair. I'll do all different kinds of things, different looks. I'm lucky that way. Some people are not good at putting on makeup, but I'm good with my own. Maybe it's from watching people put it on me for so long."[15]

But Jennifer was also comfortable shedding her glamorous image and that down-to-earth quality, combined with her natural beauty, made her a guy magnet. So it wasn't surprising that both Snipes and Harrelson shared some off-camera attraction to Jennifer. She would later reveal in an interview that both of her co-stars had made passes at her. She described Woody as being the more playful of the two but was less amused by the heavy-handed way she says Snipes came on to her. Jennifer, who was still involved with David Cruz, had no problem with Snipes's flirting, because after all, "you always flirt with your costars, its harmless."[16]

But she said Snipes wouldn't take no for an answer and the come-ons became more heavy-handed and insistent. When she continued to resist, Jennifer said he "got really upset about it. His ego was totally bruised."[17]

Her rejection caused a rift between them and Snipes didn't speak to her for two months afterwards. For her part, she thought he was simply being childish. "Actors are used to getting their way and to treating women like objects. They're so used to hearing the word *Yes.*" Typically, Jennifer didn't seem to particularly care if Snipes got upset that she had talked about the incident publicly. In fact, she found it funny. "It's time for the truth to come out!"[18]

It was also time for the film to face the critics. Overall, the reviews for Money Train were decidedly tepid, although for many critics, Jennifer was the film's saving grace. Carolyn Bingham of the Los Angeles Sentinel noted that "newcomer Jennifer Lopez as Grace Santiago, a transit cop, is stunning and gives a brilliant performance. She'll open many doors for Hispanic female actresses."[19]

Jennifer was aware that she had dodged a career bullet with Money Train. "I was the only one who came out of that movie smelling like a rose," she acknowledged.[20]

Unfortunately, the film became most remembered for a brutal crime that occurred four days after the movie's November 22, 1995, opening. In the film an arsonist sets tollbooths on fire by squirting a flammable liquid into them then igniting it. On November 26, a clerk at a Brooklyn subway station was attacked in the exact same way, suffering life-threatening burns in what appeared to be a copycat crime. Three days later on November 29, an unsuccessful attack was made at another station.

In reality, there had been similar attacks on token booths prior to the release of Money Train, and authorities had already equipped booths with flame-smothering devices. So the scenes in Money Train had been borrowed from real life, but following what were being called the Money Train attacks, Senator Bob Dole, who was expected to run for President in 1996 and who had made Hollywood morality a favorite theme, urged Americans to boycott the film during a speech on the Senate floor.

The obvious opportunistic nature of the rabble-rousing angered many involved with the film's production, including Jennifer. "It's a terrible crime, and our hearts go out to the victim," she said in an interview.[21] She also admitted the attack by Dole left her confused. "People see so many violent movies. Why would they pick that scene from Money Train? In a way, you think the film is responsible, but it's not. It's the criminals." That said, she also admitted, "It just made me more conscious of what I would do in other movies. You have such an influence over people, it's kinda scary."[22]

In a very short while, Jennifer would learn just how much a film can influence the audience that flocks to see it.

A PROFESSIONAL AND PERSONAL TURNING POINT

In May 1995, a young Tejano singer named Selena was shot and killed by the president of her fan club. Although the tragedy was a news footnote to most Anglo-Americans, in the Latino community it was a horror on par with John Lennon's murder. But even if few Hollywood executives knew who Selena was before her death, they were smart enough to smell the potential her life story might have as a drama, especially since the high-profile media coverage made Selena far more famous dead than she had been alive.

In August 1995, Selena's father, Abraham Quintanilla, issued a press release announcing that Gregory Nava, the co-writer and director of *Mi Familia*, would write and direct a movie on Selena's life. Quintanilla would serve as executive producer. There would be an international casting call to find the right actress to play Selena. For every Latina in Hollywood, it was a dream role. But initially, Jennifer didn't think she would be able to even audition for the film because she was so busy working on other movies.

At the time of the announcement she had just completed filming *Jack*, directed by Francis Ford Coppola, and was on location in Miami starring opposite Jack Nicholson and Michael Caine in *Blood and Wine*. As to why she was suddenly being hired by a Who's Who of A-list directors, Jennifer believed it was more than simple luck. "People just seem to respond to me when I go in to read for them. The same weekend Francis Ford Coppola hired me for *Jack*, and I got *Blood and Wine* after auditioning for Bob Rafelson six times. It just happens, I don't know why. There must be something you consciously do that impresses these legendary directors. It's all about controlling the emotion, you know? Anybody can scream, anybody can cry. It's about just being in the moment and doing whatever comes natural."[23]

But as her film roles improved in quality, her personal life was about to take a detour. David Cruz, her high school sweetheart and the first love of her life, became the first romantic victim of Jennifer's career—although he would not be the last. Stephanie Cozart Burton, a makeup artist on *In Living Color*, remembered Cruz as "sweet but not quite ready for prime time, like the high school boyfriend who was going to get left behind."[24]

For Jennifer it was a simple, if painful, case of two people growing in different directions. As her career moved steadily upward, Cruz, who had found work as a production assistant, seemed directionless. It was an inequity with which Jennifer could not abide. "He came out here with me and was here with me the whole time when I first started doing television. Career-wise, we weren't in the same place. He just didn't know what he wanted to do. But I had a fire under my ass. I was so fast, I was like a rocket; he was like a rock."[25]

Jennifer seemed determined not to let anything, or anyone, hold her back from realizing her dreams and pursuing her ambition. But she would discover that for all her success, finding someone to complement her life and career would be a long journey of heartbreak.

NOTES

1. "Networks on Notice Study: Latino TV characters often negative or absent." *Newsday*, September 8, 1994, p. A07.

2. Press release for Distorted Reality: Hispanic Characters in TV Entertainment, September 1, 1994.

3. Ibid.

4. Gregory Freeman. "TV Can Change the Channel on Hispanic Roles." *St. Louis Post-Dispatch*, September 9, 1994, p. 05C.

5. Ibid.

6. Dennis West. "Filming the Chicano family saga." *Cineaste, 21*, December 1, 1995, p. 26.

7. Ibid.

8. Ibid.

9. David Handleman. "A Diva is Born." *Mirabella*, July/August1998.

10. Carolyn Bingham. "Money Train' Wesley Runs Away With It." *Los Angeles Sentinel*, November 22, 1995, p. PG.

11. John Anderson. "Fall Movie Preview/November." *Entertainment Weekly*, August 25, 1995, p. 58+.

12. Carolyn Bingham. "Money Train' Wesley Runs Away With It." *Los Angeles Sentinel*, November 22, 1995, p. PG.

13. "Scene + Heard : News To Amuse: A Star-Studded Review." *In Style*, November 1, 1995, p. 40+.

14. Ibid.

15. Hillary Johnson. "Beauty Talk: Jennifer Lopez Star Of Selena." *In Style*, April 1, 1997, p. 91+.

16. Douglas Thompson. "Jennifer Lopez: The ego has landed." *Sunday Mirror*. November 15, 1998. http://www.highbeam.com/doc/1G1–60646155.html.

17. Ibid.

18. Stephen Rebello. "The Wow." *Movieline*, February 1998. http://members. aol.com/dafreshprinz/jenniferlopez/movieline0298.htm.

19. Carolyn Bingham. "Money Train' Wesley Runs Away With It." *Los Angeles Sentinel*, November 22, 1995, p. PG.

20. Ibid.

21. "On The Rise: Feeling The Heat Money Train's Jennifer Lopez Worries About Copycat Pyros." *People*, December 11, 1995, p. 157.

22. Ibid.

23. Bob Strauss. "How a former Fly Girl tackles Selena's memories, Oliver Stone's lunacy and (eeew!) giant killer snakes!" *Entertainment Online*, October 1996.

24. Ibid.

25. Stephen Rebello. "The Wow." *Movieline*, February 1998. http://members. aol.com/dafreshprinz/jenniferlopez/movieline0298.htm.

Chapter 4

ON THE RISE

While Francis Ford Coppola will forever be revered in Hollywood film history as the creative force behind the *Godfather* trilogy, his subsequent work was spotty both at the box office and artistically. So it was somewhat surprising when, in 1996, he ventured into comedy with the film *Jack*. Coppola has been called many things in the course of his career but a *laughmeister* has never been one of them. But the five-time Academy Award-winner is a director few performers will pass up an opportunity to work with. Jennifer felt honored and excited when the director chose her to play the title character's schoolteacher in the 1996 movie.

Jack can't really be described as a pure comedy, because it deals with a child who dies an untimely death. Jack's cells are growing at four times the normal rate, resulting in an accelerated maturation process. However, while his body is aging rapidly, his mental maturation is that of a normal child. By the time Jack turns ten, he looks like a full-fledged adult, played by Robin Williams. Coppola says the film is an allegory about learning the importance of tolerance and growing up too fast; of not letting our lives whiz by.

Worried that Jack will be hounded and ridiculed, his parents have Jack tutored at home. His teacher, the kindly Mr. Woodruff, gently suggests that Jack be allowed to attend public school and experience real life. Despite her misgivings, his mom takes Jack to the local school. His new teacher Miss Marquez, played by Jennifer Lopez, helps Jack and his classmates acclimate to each other. "At first, the kids are cruel to him, and afraid of him, because he's big; the size of a forty-year-old man," Jennifer explains.

"And Jack feels quite alone, because he really is just a boy. My character is there for him when he's lonely and makes sure the other kids don't pick on him. What's most fascinating to Miss Marquez is how normal Jack looks. But when you look into his eyes, you can tell he's a boy."[1]

Eventually Jack's classmates begin to appreciate him as a person. That in turns leads Jack to seize the day and live whatever time he has to the fullest. The movie ends with a grandfatherly looking 17-year-old Jack giving a life-affirming commencement address as class valedictorian.

Jack was the first time Jennifer had been cast in a film for a character not specifically written for a Latina actress. But Coppola had seen her work in My Family (My Familia) and had specifically sought Jennifer out for the crucial role of Jack's first teacher and the object of his first romantic crush. Jennifer had only praise for co-star Robin Williams, who she called "an incredible actor, as well as a brilliant comedian. He made it so easy to believe that there is a little boy hiding inside that big body. You get completely taken in."[2]

At one point, Jack develops a serious crush on his teacher. "Physically, they could probably be a great couple together," Jennifer noted, "but mentally, he's a boy and she's a grown woman." So instead of a romance, they have a meeting of the souls instead. "There are great things that happen between the two of them; tragic things, too. That's what makes the story so beautiful. It's the comedy, tragedy and the sweetness of life. The tragedy of Jack's life is that he probably will never have a romantic relationship. Miss Marquez realizes that, and it breaks her heart. It's a heart-breaking story. Jack is cheated out of a lot of things that we all get to experience in life—the joys of life."[3]

Prior to filming, Coppola invited the actors, including 15 of the young actors who played Jack's fifth-grade schoolmates, to his Napa Valley, California home for two weeks of rehearsals. Not only did it give them time to immerse themselves in their roles—the director insisted everyone stay in character for the duration of their stay—it also gave the actors time to get comfortable being around one another.

"It was an incredible experience," Jennifer recalls. "We had such a great time. It was a process I hadn't been through with any other director." But the biggest adjustment was being out in the country. "I'm a city girl, and there must have been too much clean air, or something," Jennifer laughs, "because I got a little ill."[4]

One of the hardest aspects of being an actor is to have a project that begins with such promise not reach its potential. For as wonderful as the rehearsal and filming processes were, Jack failed to ignite the passion of the audience or the critics. But just as she had with Money Train, Jennifer came away from the film richer for the experience without any taint of having been in a disappointing film.

"There are two redeeming features," John Simon wrote. "The enchanting Diane Lane as Jack's mother, and the no less enchanting Jennifer Lopez as a sympathetic teacher. But though these lovely ladies and fine actresses salvage much, it is nowhere near enough."[5]

As her notoriety on screen grew, Jennifer began lending her name to some political causes off camera. She was one of 25 executive committee members of Artists for a Democratic Victory Committee. The executive committee, which also included Maya Angelou, Barbra Streisand, William and Rose Styron, Lauren Bacall, and Rosie O'Donnell, sent a letter urging people to vote in the 1996 election and get involved in the political process. "The stakes are high this year," the letter read. "Freedom of expression, freedom of choice and the rights of privacy we cherish as Americans and artists are threatened."[6]

If there was ever a right actress making her mark at just the right political time, it was Jennifer Lopez. Not only were the film and television industries opening up their casting doors but the publishing world was also beginning to take notice of the largely untapped Latino consumer market in America. Over the next few years several big name publishers would develop divisions devoted exclusively to Hispanic personalities and magazines geared toward Latino issues—from social to cosmetic—began to appear at newsstands. Christy Haubegger, the founder of *Latina*, remembers what it was like growing up only seeing blue-eyed blonde models in magazines. "I always was a voracious magazine reader, yet I had never seen makeup articles that featured brown eyes, or almond skin."[7]

The 27-year-old Mexican American from Houston took the idea of a magazine for Latino women to over 150 prospective investors but had only raised $250,000 of the $5 million she needed to launch the magazine. The she sent her prospectus to Edward Lewis, who had started *Essence* magazine, the high-profile and very successful magazine for African-American women, years before.

"It was one of the best, most professional business proposals I've seen in twenty-five years," said Lewis to Elizabeth Llorente of *Her Latina Self*. "Haubegger is an outstanding saleswoman. She's hard-working, ethical, dedicated. She had to do this. It reminded me of myself when I was in my 20s, talking about starting *Essence*."[8]

Haubegger says Lewis was shocked "that no one had done for Hispanic women what they did for black women, that there was no comparable magazine for us."[9] It didn't take a roomful of accountants to vouch for the potential goldmine of such a publication, with more than eight million

Hispanic women living in America—a number that will only increase over the next decades.

Although when *Latina* debuted in 1996 Jennifer wasn't really a household name yet even within the Hispanic community, Haubegger's point was to show the potential young women of Latin decent could strive for, so Jennifer was asked to be the premiere issue's cover girl.

"It's important that we change the images that others have of Hispanic women," said Haubegger at the time, "but also that we present images of ourselves that are positive."[10] Despite the magazine's name, Haubegger was aware she wouldn't be able to present *only* famous Latinas on the covers because then she would only "have enough for just six magazines. Latinas are grossly underrepresented in all fields, despite the talent that's out there."[11]

But seeing Jennifer, a young woman making her way in a traditionally white industry, on the cover made Haubegger proud. "There was a beautiful Hispanic woman on the cover, Jennifer Lopez, right next to a cover with Claudia Schiffer. We'd done it. It sank in that we'd finally really, really done it."[12]

Ironically, Jennifer was too busy to spend much time pondering the social implications of her smoldering career, especially since her next film, *Blood and Wine*, would team her with two of modern cinema's most important and influential artists—who also happened to be two of Hollywood's more notorious bad boys. Director Bob Rafelson and three-time Oscar-winner Jack Nicholson are literally part of movie history and Hollywood infamy. Beginning with their collaboration on *Easy Rider* and *Five Easy Pieces*, these two old friends usually find a way to break convention while making uncompromising films that might not always work but are always interesting.

Any actor who has worked with Rafelson understands they are being directed by someone not afraid to take risks. And Rafelson seems to take secret delight in his reputation as a renegade. "I can assure you, there's nothing that I have done, there's no day in my life I can remember that has been spent entirely legally," he said once in an interview.[13]

While working on the 1980 Robert Redford film *Brubaker*, Rafelson was dismissed after allegedly beating up Twentieth Century Fox's head of production. "So much mythic energy has gone into me being this monster," Rafelson muses. "I *did* grab him, and I *did* let him go. But I did *not* hit him with thirty-seven chairs; I did not break his head open with a steel ashtray or any of the other things they had claimed I'd done."[14]

Not worried about the implications of taking on a major studio, Rafelson sued Fox for breach of contract and slander and won. "I'd like to have my impact in movies, but I don't want it to be solely based on being a crazed psychopath."[15]

With such unpredictable and volatile personalities at the helm, working on *Blood and Wine* for Jennifer was an exercise in not letting herself be intimidated. "It was incredible working with Jack. I mean he's like a legend! The first time I met him it was like: 'Oh my God! That's Jack Nicholson.' I remember the first day of rehearsal. He came in, sat down and the director wanted me to sit next to him because ours was the prominent man-woman relationship in the film. Michael Caine was sitting on the other side, and I looked at one and then the other. Then it was like I had an out-of-body experience! I wondered to myself: *What am I doing in this room with these people?* It was very scary. But fun."[16]

Blood and Wine was touted as being the last installment of a loose film trilogy that Rafelson said dealt with family problems, particularly those focusing on father-and-son relationships, with the first two films being 1970 classic *Five Easy Pieces* and *The King of Marvin Gardens*, released in 1972. In *Blood and Wine*, Nicholson is Alex Gates, a morally depleted wine dealer bowing under the weight of looming financial disaster. His marriage is crumbling, and he is embroiled in a torrid affair with a high-maintenance, luxury-loving Cuban mistress, Gabrielle, played by Jennifer. Rafelson claimed that it wasn't until Jennifer's third audition that he noticed she had a good body. It took three more times after that before he cast her.

Initially, the script called for Jennifer to engage in a steamy love scene with Nicholson. Later, Rafelson decided less would be more, opting for eroticism over sex. According to Jennifer, "Jack thought it would be sexier if we did a little salsa dancing," she recalls. "He had never danced salsa before, so I had to teach him. And you know what? He never once stepped on my toes. He's a good dancer."[17]

Despite the dark aspects of the movie, Jennifer found Miami a wonderfully exciting place to film. She enjoyed the large and lively Cuban and Hispanic communities of South Florida. She also unexpectedly found love in the most unlikely setting. While dining at Larios on the Beach, a super-hip Miami Beach Cuban restaurant co-owned by singer Gloria Estefan, Jennifer was smitten by one of the waiters. She turned to her best friend Arlene, who by then was also working as her assistant, and announced, "That's the man I'm going to marry."[18] Arlene says she took one look at Ojani Noa and knew Jennifer meant it. However it would take a while before Jennifer would actually be introduced to Noa, who was a recent émigré from Cuba.

Now that she had her sights set on the handsome waiter, Jennifer wasn't interested in dating anyone else—a fact that upset her *Blood and Wine* co-star Stephen Dorff, who had developed a serious crush on Jennifer. Jennifer admits she flirted with Dorff a little but didn't really encourage him. So she was disappointed when he began sulking and stopped talking to her. She finally told him not to "pull a Wesley on me!"[19] after which he gave up.

Jennifer kept her sights firmly on her waiter and became a regular at Larios. But she was still too shy to approach Noa, in part because she felt her Spanish wasn't very good. Jennifer admits that to catch Noa's eye, she did "everything in the book. I would go see him at the restaurant where he waited tables all the time and walk past him to the bathroom a million times. One time, he was coming my way, and I slipped. I was so mortified! He was like, 'Careful.'"[20]

Finally, Jennifer's girlfriend took matters in her own hands and arranged for them to be seated at one of Noa's tables. "That night," Jennifer recalls wistfully, "we went out, and it was mad love from that point on."[21]

It was the beginning of a passionate romance that Jennifer thought at the time would last forever. Life was so good it was scary—not only was her career blooming but she was also in love. The combination gave her more confidence than ever and perhaps allowed her to see things in a new way.

For example, despite her initial feelings of professional awe working with Nicholson, Jennifer would curiously take a harsher stand later, calling Nicholson "a legend in his own time and in his own mind—like the rest of us are peons."[22] Perhaps in retrospect, the sting of the first negative reviews she had suffered in her young movie career colored her feelings.

Robert Denerstein of *The Rocky Mountain News* observed, "Rafelson infuses *Blood and Wine* with a purposefully exhausted quality, as if these characters are ready to drop in their tracks. The climate is desperate and more than a little depraved, which means the movie works but isn't a great deal of fun, except for watching Nicholson and Caine trying to out-sleaze each other . . . But the junior members of the sleazoid firm (Dorff and Lopez) aren't quite up to speed. Early on, Jennifer allows a Charo-like accent to turn her character into a bit of a caricature."[23]

While it might be a cliché to say more is learned from failure than success, it also happens to be true. Reading comments that questioned her ability made Jennifer burn inside and rather than hang her head, she couldn't wait to go out and make those same critics eat their words. She already signed on to her next film, this time an action-adventure yarn called *Anaconda*.

When Will Smith was trying to go from rap-artist-turned-television-star into a big screen leading man, he took a look at the then-biggest box office hits in Hollywood history. What jumped out at him was that by and large, it was sci-fi and action adventure flicks that drew the biggest audiences. That's what led to him star in *Independence Day*, the film that made Smith one of the top movie dogs in the business.

While Jennifer Lopez wasn't as pointedly calculating as Smith in her selection of film roles, it was always her mindset that she wanted to show she could do different types of roles in whatever genre was presented to her. So taking on a thriller after the emotional heaviness of *Blood and Wine* seemed like a natural career choice, even though at first glance *Anaconda* (1997) may not have seemed like the smartest choice. But rather than try to present itself as any kind of modern classic, *Anaconda* reveled in the B-movie kitschiness of it all. The real star of the film was a 40-foot-long animatronic snake that slithered and stalked through the film like a land-locked great white.

As Lisa Schwarzbaum aptly noted in *Entertainment Weekly*, "With its direct-to-video-type title, it's the kind of retro, eek! eek! production that studios don't often make anymore, now that movies about tornadoes and invasions by aliens have become too expensive to be taken humorously by the companies that foot the bills. The makers of *Anaconda* appear to have no such qualms. Without winking, like *Scream,* at its own provenance, the story is a blurry clone of *Jaws*, which is to say *Moby Dick*, which is to say the battle between an obsessive loner and his amoral quarry, during which everybody in the neighborhood suffers."[24]

The premise of the film is familiar to anyone who's ever seen a nature vs. civilization scarefest. In a throwback to yesteryear, director Luis Llosa shot the film in the wide-screen CinemaScope format. The predictable story follows a young documentary team led by director Terri Flores, played by Jennifer Lopez, and her crew, which included the unlikely pairing of Eric Stoltz as scientific advisor Dr. Steven Cale and yet another rapper-turned-actor, Ice Cube as Danny the cameraman. Jon Voight co-stars as the outrageously over-the-top villain, a Paraguayan priest turned serpent expert cum poacher named Paul Sarone. He approached the role with scenery-chewing gusto.

Flores and her team are in the jungle to shoot a movie about the mysterious "people of the mist," an elusive tribe that is said to worship various deadly snakes that populate the river. While searching for the tribe, they find Sarone living on a rickety boat and take him on board. Of course, he immediately sets about terrorizing everyone and sucks the team into participating in his great Ahab-esque obsession—finding the legendary 40-foot anaconda. He is determined to capture the snake alive and take him back to civilization where fame and glory will then await him. Apparently, Sarone's never seen *King Kong*. . . .

To aid in his quest, he offers members of the team as living bait, except for Dr. Cale who is debilitated early on after a run-in with a particularly nasty insect. During his quest, Sarone also destroys a nest of baby snakes, bringing out the mother bear in the snake, as it were. Soon the hunted becomes the hunter. Of course, no thriller would be complete without the required turns of bad luck—the radio stops working, they lose their boat fuel, and one of the team members is badly injured. Finally, the snake makes its presence known and the body count rapidly starts to mount. The anaconda eventually wreaks its revenge on Sarone by swallowing him whole—then regurgitating him so everyone can see his death throes. At that point Terri Flores promptly blows Mr. Slither to high rain forest heaven.

One way in which *Anaconda* does not follow the recipe of a typical horror yarn is that the good guys are people of color with Lopez and Ice Cube as the co-heroes of the movie. Although not a snake lover, the rapper says he was attracted to the film because he thought it symbolic. "Political snakes are pretty much the same as the kind of snakes we deal with in this movie. So, I knew what I was going to be dealing with; these snakes are just coming from a different angle."[25]

For Jennifer, starring in an action film gave her a chance to show off her natural athleticism. "I try to do a lot of my own stunts and everybody says it's stupid, especially actors who have been in the business a long time," she commented at the time. "They say, 'What, are you stupid? That's what a stunt double is for.'" But Jennifer brushed aside such concerns. "If I can, if it's not too dangerous, I'll do it. For me, the action stuff in this kind of movie is fun. I'm very athletic and agile, too, so that all helps. I don't look stupid doing the moves. You know, some women are not good for that; they're good actresses, but they're not good for the physical stuff. You have to be able to sell that. They have to believe you could actually hold your own."[26]

Jennifer admitted, though, that "I got pretty bruised up. They're tough to do. It's hard on your body to do those things twelve, fourteen hours a day, but I love it. I would be an action star—if I had the opportunity—in a minute."[27]

Later, she would tell Dennis Hensley of *Cosmopolitan*, "I'm tough that way. Some actresses are like, 'Get my stunt double, I don't want to have to run.' But I'll do anything. They have pictures of me doing the fittings at night for *Selena* while I was filming *Anaconda*. I was like the Elephant Woman from the hips down. It was a major bruise movie."[28]

But Jennifer went into the shoot knowing it was would more physically demanding than any role she'd tackled. "When I read the script, I knew what I was getting into. When we were negotiating my money, actually I said, 'What? They don't want to give me THAT? Do they know that I'm going to be wet, bloody, tied up . . .?' I said, 'This is no good. They've got to give me more money,'" she said jokingly. "No, I knew it would be tough from the beginning, but I also liked the fact that it would be a strong woman character who is idealistic and has all of this stuff thrown at her, and she rises to the occasion. The fact that we have a woman heroine was very appealing."[29]

Unfortunately, a majority of critics found the film less than appetizing. But there was once a study that stated the obvious—scathing critical reviews don't seem to have any significant affect on a film's box office, and *Anaconda* must have been one of their prime examples. On its opening weekend in April 1997 the film took in $16.6 million in ticket sales earning the number one spot at the box office. Part of *Anaconda's* appeal was that it was the only new special-effects film in release at the time, with the studios saving their big-budget spectacles for summer. The other draw was the one-two punch of Lopez and Ice Cube that drew in young people. Defying critics and surpassing even the highest hopes of the studio, *Anaconda* stayed among the top box office leaders for seven weeks.

Suddenly, Jennifer was being seen as more than just a talented actress; she was becoming an acknowledged box office draw. If there were any lingering doubts as to her rising status in the Hollywood pecking order, Lopez was about to erase them.

NOTES

1. Thomas C. Fleming. "Bill Cosby/Jennifer Lopez in 'Jack.'" *The Sun Reporter*, August 8, 1996, p. PG.

2. Ibid.

3. Ibid.

4. Ibid.

5. John Simon. "Tin Cup" [movie reviews]. *National Review*, 48, September 16, 1996, p. 67.

6. Jeannie Williams. "Wishing upon stars to help Democrats." *USA Today*, July 26, 1996, p. 02D.

7. Anita McDivitt. "New women's magazine uses a different tone." *The Dallas Morning News*, June 26, 1996, p. 5C.

8. Elizabeth Llorente. "Her Latina Self." *The Record* (Bergen County, NJ), July 21, 1996, p. 101.

9. Anita McDivitt. "New women's magazine uses a different tone." *The Dallas Morning News*, June 26, 1996, p. 5C.

10. Ibid.

11. Elizabeth Llorente. "Her Latina Self." *The Record* (Bergen County, NJ), July 21, 1996, p. l01.

12. Ibid.

13. Howard Feinstein. "Bob And Jack's Excellent Adventures." *Newsday*, February 2, 1997, p. C08.

14. Ibid.

15. Ibid.

16. Martin Palmer. *Total Film*, December 1998. http://www.beyond-beautiful. org/topic/3207/t/Total-Film-December-1998.html.

17. AP wire service press release, March 3, 1997.

18. Martha Frankel. "Love In Bloom." *In Style*, Mary 1, 1997, p. 196.

19. Stephen Rebello. "The Wow." *Movieline*, February 1998. http://members. aol.com/dafreshprinz/jenniferlopez/movieline0298.htm.

20. Dennis Hensley. "How do you say "hot" in Spanish?" *Cosmopolitan, 222*, April 1, 1997, p. 190.

21. Ibid.

22. Douglas Thompson. "Jennifer Lopez: The ego has landed." *Sunday Mirror*, November 15, 1998. http://www.highbeam.com/doc/1G1–60646155.html.

23. Robert Denerstein. "Taste Of 'Blood And Wine' Is A Bitter One." *Denver Rocky Mountain News*, March 14, 1997, p. 7D.

24. Lisa Schwarzbaum. "This Mortal Coil 'Anaconda' Squeezes Out Some Big B-Movie Moments." *Entertainment Weekly*, April 18, 1997, p. 48.

25. *Anaconda* press kit, mailed to journalists in April 1997.

26. Ibid.

27. Bob Strauss. "Blood and Guts." *Chicago Sun-Times*, February 16, 1997. http://www.highbeam.com/doc/1P2–4374767.html.

28. Dennis Hensley. "How do you say 'hot' in Spanish?" *Cosmopolitan, 222*, April 1, 1997, p. 190.

29. Patrick Stoner. *Flicks*, April 1997. Available at http://www.whyy.org/tv12/ flicksinterviews.html.

Chapter 5

A TEJANO TRAGEDY

Prior to 1995, few Americans outside the Latino community really knew much about Selena Quintanilla-Pérez. But after her murder in the spring of that year, the outpouring of grief by her fans drew attention to a phenom who was surprisingly unknown by most of white America. Perhaps more than any other single event, the media attention Selena's death brought to bear on the Hispanic-American community reflected a subculture that few in white American had ever paid much attention to. That someone like Selena could have been so successful, so beloved and so talented and yet be almost unknown to the general masses was almost as shocking as her untimely death. And perhaps most tragically ironic is that Selena died before she had the opportunity to try and "cross over" to mainstream stardom; however, Jennifer's portrayal of Selena in the film would propel *her* past the cultural divide and make Jennifer the most successful cross-over female Latin star in Hollywood.

Selena was born in Lake Jackson, Texas, a blue-collar town not far from Houston. She lived with her two older siblings and her parents, Abraham, Jr., and Marcela Quintanilla. Although her father had a good job working at Dow Chemical as a shipping clerk, he was at heart a frustrated musician. In his younger days, he had sung with a popular South Texas band called *Los Dinos* and never lost his passion for music and performing. So when Selena started singing around six years old, he began to fantasize about making her a star. Ironically, though, Selena showed little interest in Latin music of any kind, instead preferring Motown, pop, and country.

It's been variously reported that her father either quit his job at Dow or was laid off. Whatever the case, Abraham stopped working at Dow and opened up a restaurant in 1980. For entertainment, he had his three children—Selena, her brother Abraham III, and sister Suzette—perform for the patrons. But a year later the restaurant went bankrupt. Like many small businesses in Texas at the time, they were undercut by the sudden downturn of the Texas oil industry. Not only did Abraham lose the restaurant, he lost the family home as well. "That's when we began our musical career," Selena later recalled. "We had no alternative."[1]

The Quintanilla family moved to Corpus Christi and it was there that they became involved with the music business. "We went to Corpus Christi to put food on the table when I was six-and-a-half," Selena said. "We would play for family weddings. When I was eight I recorded my first song in Spanish, a country song. When I was nine we started a Tex-Mex band."[2]

And at only nine years old, Selena went on the road with her family band, which Abraham named *Selena y Los Dinos*—Selena and the Guys—which included her elder siblings and guitarist Chris Pérez. They performed a musical style called Tejano, a bright, up-tempo Spanish-language blend of Tex-Mex rhythms, pop-style tunes, and German polka that is hugely popular in Mexico and the Southwest. Sometimes Tejano is also called Tex-Mex or *conjunto*. The history of the genre goes back to the turn of the twentieth century, when Mexican-Americans put on country dances. Couples twirled and spun to a polka-like beat played on accordions and big Bajo Sexto guitars, which are still the main instruments when playing Tejano.

Like any local band scraping to get by, they played anywhere, anytime, singing from roadhouse dance halls to weddings. "If we got 10 people in one place, that was great," Selena said. "We ate a lot of hamburgers and shared everything."[3]

Although to some kids, traveling around in a beat-up family band might sound like a fanciful adventure, for Selena it was a hard-scrabble reality. Selena never got to experience high school, having dropped out in the eighth grade. So going out for pizza after the football games and proms were things she only heard about but would never enjoy firsthand. "I lost a lot of my teenage period," she acknowledged. "But I got a lot out of it too. I was more mature."[4] It was typical of Selena's upbeat nature to dwell on the positive rather than obsess over the negative.

Over the next six years, the band attracted a following and earned more profitable gigs. They released over 10 albums during that time. But their lives, and Serena's career, changed abruptly in 1987 after Selena won the Tejano Music Awards for female vocalist and performer of the year. At only 15 years old she emerged as the bright, new star in Tejano.

Two years later, EMI Latin president Josa Behar signed *Selena y Los Dinos* to a record deal.

As she matured, Selena developed a personal fashion style that became her trademark—red lipstick, long, brightly colored fingernails, tight pants, bustiers, and stomach-revealing midriffs. Between her clothes and her high-energy performances, Selena earned the apt nickname of the "Tex-Mex madonna." It was a persona her father, a Jehovah's Witness, grew ever more disapproving of, but one he could do little about. To Selena, it was simply part of the act. "What I do on stage, you won't catch me doing off stage," she explained once. "Deep down, I'm still kind of timid and modest. On stage, I let go. Besides, she added, I love shiny things and I love clothing."[5]

That wasn't the only contradiction about Selena. The biggest irony was that this new Princess of Latin pop could barely speak a lick of Spanish. After her brother A. J. wrote the songs, she learned the lyrics phonetically. It wasn't until she signed with EMI that she started taking Spanish lessons, although she never really developed any kind of fluency with the language. She did, however, maintain her Texas drawl.

It seemed that anyone who saw Selena perform became smitten, so her legion of fans grew steadily. After seeing one of her concerts in San Antonio, Texas, which is considered the Mecca for Tejano, a registered nurse by the name of Yolanda Saldivar was so taken by the singer that she was inspired to start an official fan club. She approached Abraham, who had repeatedly turned down other such offers in the past; Abraham wasn't the kind to let such matters be out of his control. But Yolanda didn't seem like your usual fan club personality. She was older and had a steady job. Although she had no children and had never married—for that mattered, she apparently never dated, either—she had taken custody of her brother's children after he abandoned them. Perhaps most importantly, her niece was a childhood friend of Selena's. All that plus her unbridled enthusiasm for Selena won over Abraham, who gave her the unpaid honor of establishing Selena's official fan club.

A fan club was no small matter to Selena, who once observed, "Fan clubs can ruin you if people get upset and turned off by them."[6] So she was very pleased with the way hers was going and felt Yolanda was doing an exceptional job. When membership grew to 9,000 in four years, Selena was impressed enough to put Saldivar in charge of finances for the club. Soon, Selena began to consider Yolanda one of her closest friends. It was a show of trust that would eventually prove fatal.

By the time she was 21, Selena was a millionaire and the most popular star in Tejano music. Where she once sang to a roomful of roadside diners, she now performed for crowds as large as 60,000. Thanks to her popularity, annual sales of Tejano music soared between 1990 and 1995 from below $7 million annually to over $35 million. Many major recording labels, including Sony, EMI, Fonovisa, Rodven, WEA Latina, and Arista set up Tejano divisions after Selena broke onto the scene.

Seemingly overnight, Selena had gone from living hand to mouth with her family, to being the million dollar family breadwinner. And her personal life was going equally as well. She had fallen in love with her band's guitar player, Chris Pérez, and the two were quietly married in 1992. Abraham was concerned that Selena's marriage would both turn away her young male admirers as well as taint her youthful image. It did neither. In fact, her popularity just continued to grow because for as much as people loved her music, they seemed to love Selena the person even more. Although she came from conservative, traditional parents, Selena was as outgoing and friendly as any average Texan. Her down-to-earth qualities kept her close to her roots; instead of moving to Houston or San Antonio she continued living in her old Corpus Christi neighborhood—although she did splurge and buy herself a bright red Porsche.

In 1994, Selena took a major step up the music ladder by winning a Grammy for best Mexican-American album, *Selena Live*. By the spring of 1995, her next album, *Amor Prohibido* (Forbidden Love), had sold over a half million copies domestically. Altogether, her five EMI releases had sold an estimated three million copies worldwide. "Never in my dreams would I have thought that I would become this big," she said. "I am still freaking out."[7]

Like so many Latin performers before her, Selena was a success mainstream America knew little about. The biggest drawback to cross-over success for Selena was the same bugaboo that later plagued Ricky Martin and other Latin artists—the great language divide. Anglo audiences want to hear music in English. However, in the way that Gloria Estefan had made American radio airwaves safe for Cuban sounds, EMI believed Selena could do for Tejano, which is why Selena's next project was going to be recorded in English. Selena was also stretching her wings and dabbling in other areas such as acting, having appeared in the film *Don Juan DeMarco*, with Marlon Brando and Johnny Depp.

In the summer of 1994, Selena made a fateful decision. She promoted Yolanda Saldivar to a full-time paid employee in charge of a new business venture dubbed Selena Etc. Inc. Selena, who had always been in love with fashions and style, had opened boutiques in Corpus Christi and San Antonio. The shops sold a line of Selena brand clothes and jewelry and offered hair styling and manicure—a kind of one-stop primp and shopping for the Tejano girl on the go. Selena Etc. Inc. was formed to handle merchandising its products to other stores.

Although Yolanda had proven herself to be a hard worker, she was in way over her head. Her new position called for her to deal with people directly on a daily business and her people skills were in low supply. Designer Martin Gomez, who Selena had hired to help produce the clothing lines, says he had nothing but problems with Yolanda. "From the beginning there was such tension between Yolanda and myself. She was mean, she was manipulative." So much so that Gomez quit in January 1995. "I told Selena I was scared of Yolanda," he claims. "She wouldn't let me talk to Selena anymore. She was very possessive."[8]

Selena apparently failed to confront Yolanda about the situation with Gomez but soon other disturbing reports started filtering in. Abraham received complaints from fans who claimed they had sent in their $22 membership but never received any of the promotional items that were supposed to accompany membership, such as T-shirts and CDs. Selena's father did question Yolanda, who insisted it was just a bookkeeping error.

In early March several employees told Selena they suspected Saldivar of embezzling money from the company—forging checks and taking money instead of paying bills. This time Selena had no choice but to finally confront her friend. It was an ugly scene, during which Saldivar vehemently maintained her innocence and said she could prove it. But weeks went by and she still had not provided any exonerating documentation.

A few days before the murder, Saldivar claimed she had been kidnapped while in Laredo. She said she had been raped and beaten and that her car had been stolen. In the car had been the financial documentation proving her innocence. When Selena arrived at the Days Inn motel where Saldivar was staying, she reportedly insisted on driving Yolanda to a nearby hospital for medical treatment. Before doctors began their examination, Saldivar admitted the story was a lie. It was at that point that Selena knew she had to sever her ties with Saldivar, who realized the end of her association with the singer was near.

On Thursday, March 30, Yolanda called Selena. She suggested they discuss the matter in person and asked her to come to the Days Inn motel where she was staying. She also told her to come alone. Instead, Selena brought her husband Chris but the meeting proved fruitless.

The following morning Selena returned to the Days Inn, this time alone, after Saldivar called to say she had found bank books and checks that would prove her innocence. According to eyewitnesses, shortly before noon a screaming Selena burst out of Room 158 hysterically screaming for help. A motel maid said she looked up and saw Saldivar shoot Selena in the back.[9]

The bullet from the .38 caliber revolver hit Selena in the upper back but she still managed to make it to the lobby before collapsing. At 11:50 A.M. police received a 911 call reporting a shooting at the motel. Selena managed to remain conscious long enough to say Yolanda had shot her. Paramedics rushed the critically wounded singer to Memorial Medical Center while authorities notified the family. At the hospital, a team of doctors worked to save Selena's life, including transfusing five pints of blood—against the wishes of her father's Jehovah's Witness faith. But it was a moot point. The bullet had severed an artery and Selena was pronounced dead at 1:05 P.M.

Police responding to the scene surrounded Saldivar in her pickup truck but she held them at bay, holding the gun to her head and threatening suicide. According to Corpus Christi Assistant Police Chief Ken Bung, Saldivar expressed remorse throughout the standoff. Finally, after 10 hours, she surrendered and was placed under arrest for the murder of Selena Quintanilla-Pérez.

As word of the shooting spread, fans reacted with deep grief and shock. For the Mexican-American community, it was as devastating as John Lennon's murder had been. Hundreds of grief stricken fans gathered at the Days Inn, drawn by the tragedy and by the need to see for themselves. Across town, shell-shocked fans paid silent homage driving or walking by Selena's modest house, where some left bouquets of flowers, balloons, and notes of condolence against the chain-link fence.

Not only was her loss mourned, but also her never-to-be-realized potential. Selena was vastly talented, deeply adored. "This was not some sexy babe groomed by a record company," said respected music critic Enrique Fernandez. "We'll never be sure of how far she could have gone."[10]

Cameron Randle of Arista/Texas agreed. "Selena was not merely forging an exceptional career, she was defining a new genre as uniquely American as Delta blues or New Orleans jazz . . . She was about to take center stage as the first Tejano performer to attempt a full-scale crossover. And she was robbed of that opportunity."[11]

Indeed, Selena's cross-over album, *Dreaming of You*, would posthumously spawn two hit ballads—"I Could Fall in Love" and "Dreaming of You." The fact they were among the last songs she recorded in her short life simply added to the poignancy of the loss.

The outpouring of grief over Selena's death, just two weeks before her 24th birthday, caught many Americans by surprise. They watched in stunned amazement as thousands and thousands of fans, as many as

50,000 from America, Mexico, and even Canada, converged on Bayfront Plaza Convention Center in Corpus Christi, Texas, to pay their last respects and say goodbye to the young singer. They laid white long-stemmed roses on her closed coffin, unaware that inside, Selena was going to the grave the way she had entertained her audiences, with bright red lipstick and freshly painted fingernails, wearing a purple gown. In San Antonio, other unofficial memorials were held and the Tejano radio stations conducted Selena marathons in her honor.

Yolanda Saldivar was convicted of murder, although she maintains to this day she was really just trying to kill herself. She also claims to be a victim of jealousy from others who wanted to be as close to Selena as she was. While Selena's father believes Yolanda killed his daughter in cold blood out of fear she was about to get caught embezzling, others suspect her motivation was more desperate. Esmeralda Garza, who knew Yolanda, says, "Saldivar could have been fired by Selena and gone and gotten her old job back. She was doing well as a nurse. She probably couldn't accept the fact that she wasn't going to be around Selena anymore."[12]

At Saldivar's trial, defense attorney Douglas Tinker argued that Yolanda was so upset by the accusations of theft that she actually meant to kill herself but accidentally shot Selena instead. The jury didn't believe it and Saldivar was sentenced to life in prison.[13]

It is one thing to play an historical figure long dead. It's quite another to portray someone who still lives vividly in the minds of those who knew them. As she immersed herself into the life of Selena, Jennifer Lopez became increasingly aware of the challenge she faced in doing justice to someone so beloved and in capturing the essence that made Selena so loved. "This movie is the celebration of the life of an amazing person," Jennifer observed while working on the film. "Selena was someone who had not just tremendous talent but also a beautiful heart and I think that's what her fans loved most about her. I knew her memory's still fresh in their minds, so the most important thing for me is to get it right."[14] But before she could completely delve into the skin of Selena, she had to go big game hunting first.

NOTES

1. Bill Hewitt, Joseph Harmes, and Bob Stewart. "Before Her Time." *People*, April 17, 1995, p. 48+. http://www.selenalareina.com/bio.html.

2. Ibid.

3. Ibid.

4. Robert Seidenberg. "Legacy Requiem For A Latin Star." *Entertainment Weekly*, April 14, 1995, p. 20.

5. Ibid.

6. Ibid.

7. "The Crime: Fatal Attraction Fired By The Singer She Adored, Selena's Biggest Fan May Have Turned Deadly." *People*, May 5, 1995, p. 59+.

8. Ibid.

9. Ibid.

10. Robert Seidenberg. "Legacy Requiem for a Latin Star." *Entertainment Weekly*, April 14, 1995, p. 20.

11. Ibid.

12. Ibid.

13. "Woman Who Murdered Singer Gets a Sentence of Life in Prison." New York Times, October 27, 1995. Available at http://query.nytimes.com/gst/fullpage. html?res=990CE6D61639F934A15753C1A963958260&scp=2&sq=%22Yolanda+ saldivar%22&st=nyt.

14. "The Making of Selena." *Hispanic*, March 31, 1997, p. PG.

Chapter 6

A CAREER-MAKING ROLE

From the beginning, the Selena film project was a high profile property and the production would ultimately be filled with as much drama off-camera as there was on screen. The first roles to be cast were the most pivotal—Selena and her father, Abraham Quintanilla. Their relationship in many ways was the underlying foundation of why Selena became who she did and would also serve as the source of emotional and dramatic conflict in the film. In addition to the grown-up Selena, director Gregory Nava also needed a girl to play the younger Selena, a role that eventually went to an unknown actress from South Texas, Becky Lee Meza, then 10.

When the casting call first went out in March 1996 for a young woman to play Selena, Abraham Quintanilla and the other producers made a point of saying they were willing to hire an unknown to play the doomed singer. Young women from all over the country flooded the production office with pictures and singing tapes in hopes of being the cinematic Cinderella. Open calls were held in San Antonio, Los Angeles, Miami, and Chicago, and an estimated 22,000 aspirants were screened. But from the outset, the deck was really stacked in Jennifer's favor, if for no other reason that director Gregory Nava was familiar with her work and considered her one of Hollywood's brightest young actresses, frequently singing her praises in interviews.

Ironically, though, it wasn't a role that immediately grabbed Jennifer. "I got a call saying that Gregory Nava was going to direct the Selena story," she recalls. "Now, I knew she was about my age and they might be considering me for it. But it wasn't this thing like, 'I have to get this part.'"[1]

It wasn't until Jennifer went on the audition that her mild interest turned into determination. "That's when I realized that there was all the dancing and singing, and then I got really excited about it."[2]

According to the director, she nailed the audition, which required her to perform nine minutes of concert scenes and emote eight pages of script. "There's no way you can put a character together for an audition," Jennifer maintains. "But you can give the idea of whether you have the required charisma and the ability to do it."[3]

Jennifer acknowledges many of the young women who auditioned probably looked more like Selena than she did, "But I believe [the producers] were trying to find somebody to capture who Selena was; what she was like inside and why she was such a special person. She was happy. She loved life, and she loved what she did. She worked with her family and had great family values. She embraced her culture."[4]

Some established actresses might have taken offense at having to audition against unknowns for a role, but Jennifer took the casting requirements in stride. "I'm still at the stage of my career where I have to go after things that I want," she said at the time. "It would be stupid not to. Even if I was at the caliber of Sandra Bullock or Michelle Pfeiffer or Julia Roberts, if there was a role I wanted, I'd say, 'Can I come in and read for that?' That's how you get to do the good roles. You can't let it get offered to everyone else before it comes to you."[5]

At the final callbacks in Los Angeles, Jennifer came face-to-face with Selena's father, who had final casting approval. Jennifer says his presence added a surreal atmosphere to the audition. "He was standing in the doorway, and I was overcome by this weird feeling. I blocked him from my field of vision, and used the uncomfortable feeling of him being there when I talked about him in the scene. The proof is in the pudding, and I knew I had to make good pudding that day."[6]

Abraham had an unusual amount of control for a first time producer, and his prominent role in the making of the film fueled criticism that certain elements of Selena's life had been whitewashed to make the family patriarch come off in a more appealing light. But from the beginning, Quintanilla had insisted that the stars of the film and the majority of the production team be Hispanic. He hand-picked Nava to direct and co-produced the film with Esparza/Katz Productions, headed by Moctezuma Esparza and Bob Katz.

Nava denied that Abraham dictated the creative thrust of the film in any way. "Abraham is the consummate father. He knew if he didn't make this movie, someone would, and it would be exploitive stuff," the director explained. "He made this movie to preserve his daughter's memory; it's a work of love. He may have been hands-on but he knows when to let people do their job."[7]

The budget for Selena was $18 million; a very modest film by Hollywood standards but the biggest budget Nava had ever worked with. With money to spend, Nava was able to attract an experienced production team. He could also afford to hire experienced actors including Jon Seda to portray Chris Perez. But in an interesting touch, some members of Selena's band played themselves: singer/songwriter Pete Astudillo, writer Rick Vela, and keyboard player Art Meza.

Edward James Olmos, the dean of Latin actors, was hired to play Abraham Quintanilla. He is often crediting with being among the first to break Hispanic stereotypes in Hollywood. In films including Zoot Suit and Stand and Deliver, for which he earned an Academy Award nomination, Olmos forced producers to rethink the way they were casting Latinos. But at the time Selena was filmed he still lamented the paucity of good Hispanic roles and projects. "Latinos in Hollywood have been here forever, but have never really been able to cross into making American films of Latin themes marketable or profitable."[8]

Jennifer agreed with Olmos and knew her career was floating on rarified Hollywood air. "I'm fortunate because I've built up a little body of work," she acknowledged. "Still, there aren't a lot of parts for us and we're not generally considered for other roles that aren't race specific. It's starting to change a little bit, but we're still treated like foreigners who just got here because we're not white." But she added pointedly, "We're as American as they come!"[9]

Jennifer believes Latinos bear some of the responsibility for how the status quo developed by not being pushy enough. "African-Americans banded together and said this was something they were going to do, and I think it's something the Latino community has to do, too. We need to realize there is strength in numbers, and if we say we're going to write our own stories and do our own things, then we can force our way in."[10] Jennifer had certainly done her part: with Selena, she became the highest-paid Latina actress in Hollywood history.

Gregory Nava and Abraham Quintanilla held a press conference on June 18, 1996 to present the two actresses who would portray Selena. Nava described Becky Lee Meza as a young actress who showed "tremendous promise. Just as Selena's talent and star quality catapulted her to the top of the music industry, Becky captivated us. To stand out from such an enormous field shows just how much natural talent and ability she displayed."[11]

Jennifer acknowledged the film was bound to be emotional. "It's a very touchy subject. She didn't pass away very long ago, and she's so fresh in everybody's minds, and that makes it a huge challenge to play her. Even people who didn't remember her now know what she was like, how she acted. They know everything about her. People are going to be looking at me with a critical eye and, definitely, I feel that. But to me, it's a challenge. Actresses are always complaining there are no challenging roles, but here's one of those roles."[12]

Usually, press conferences such as these are conducted in a festive kind of atmosphere but on this day the air was understandably subdued. As Nava noted, "To be perfectly honest, this is a movie that I wish I wasn't making."[13] What the director didn't reveal that day was how hard he fought to get Jennifer the role. "I won't name names, but Warner Brothers was talking to other types to play Selena," Nava later admitted, pointing out it wasn't the first time he had gone to bat for Jennifer. "When I made *Mi Familia*, the studio, New Line, wanted to cast non-Latinas because there weren't any Latina 'names.' I said no, and I fought hard."[14]

To prepare for the role, Jennifer did more than just watch tapes and listen to recordings; she literally immersed herself into Selena's daily life. She moved in with Selena's sister in Corpus Christi, Texas, and spent time with the rest of the family, especially Marcella. "She told me I was just like Selena," Jennifer said of the singer's mother. 'You never eat, you don't want to look fat, you never drink enough water! You're just like Selena.'"[15]

Jennifer grew close to the Quintanillas, who in turn opened their hearts, photos albums, and videotapes to Jennifer. "I think anyone who does a film like this about a real person, you have to do your homework," she explains, "and find every insight into who she was and what made her tick, and what was the flaw in her personality that led to her death."[16]

Initially, Jennifer had intended to talk at length with Selena's husband, Chris Pérez, but once in Texas, she found herself unwilling to intrude on what she perceived to be his continued grief. "I thought I was a reminder for him and I just didn't want to go there . . . I talked more often with Abraham, Marcella, Suzanne, the rest of the family and friends. Of course, they have different views. Obviously, she was a wife to one person, a lover, and to Abraham, she was his little girl."[17]

It was Jennifer's job to coalesce all those views into a living person on screen. Although movie make-up could make Jennifer look more like Selena physically, it wasn't impersonation she was after. "I wanted to capture her personality, down to the tiniest details—even the way she rubbed her nose." But the more she got into the role, the more the tragedy of it all weighed on her. "As I'm researching it, I just sit there and cry."[18]

Selena exhibited a beauty and body type not often seen among mainstream pop stars—instead of being waifish she was voluptuous and curvy.

So even though Jennifer needed to be in good shape for the rigors of film-ing, she also had to be careful not to overdo it. "When I first went in for a [wardrobe] fitting the director told me he was concerned, and I thought, 'Oh no. I'm too fat.' Instead he said, 'Selena didn't really have stomach muscles and you might be getting too buff.'"[19]

Selena's comfort with her womanly body touched a nerve in Jennifer. Being an actress in Hollywood, Jennifer knew first hand that a woman with any kind of voluptuousness was going against the status quo. "I've always had trouble with wardrobe people!" she admits. "I don't have the typical very straight body. I'm hippy. I have a big butt. It's not like you can hide it. But when I get in with the wardrobe designer . . . they're always trying to minimize because we see all those actresses who are so thin and white. So I'm like, 'This is my shape. This is my body.' In Selena, though, it was the other way around: 'How can we shoot her butt so it looks like Selena's,'" Jennifer laughs.[20]

Most of the time, film actors work in a creative vacuum; they get no immediate fan feedback and have to wait months before finding out if the audience liked the work they did. But when Jennifer filmed the concert scenes, she understood the addictive drug that performing live in front of thousands of adoring fans could be.

For one scene, Nava assembled over thirty thousand fans in the Houston Astrodome to recreate a concert held February 26, 1995, during the Hous-ton Livestock Show and Rodeo, one of the biggest concerts of her career. The most nerve-wracking part for Jennifer was wondering if Selena's fans would accept her. Some Hispanic advocacy groups complained about an actor of Puerto Rican descent being cast to portray a Mexican American. Jennifer was also aware that some in the Latin media were offended because she didn't speak Spanish very well. Of course, Jennifer pointed out, "Selena didn't either!"[21] Jennifer quickly realized that she couldn't pay attention to any of the criticism. "I said, 'This is going to interfere with my performance. I can't get wrapped up in this. I can't read papers. I can't watch news. I have to do this part.' So I went about my work."[22]

Gregory Nava admitted the criticism felt like a kind of betrayal by people who should have been the most supportive. "It was a little hurtful. They should be celebrating that we have an all-Latino cast and that Jennifer Lopez, one of our own, is becoming a star."[23]

With all the controversy, Jennifer had no idea what the reception would be. She even worried out loud about being booed. But as soon as Jennifer stepped on stage, the roar from the crowd was deafening. Most surpris-ing to Jennifer was the fact that many were calling out *Jennifer* instead of *Selena*. Once she was basking in the audience's passionate response, her worries dissolved. For a full 90 minutes, everyone in the Astrodome stood on their feet and cheered her every Selena-like move. "It was an incredible rush," Jennifer says. "I felt a lot of love from that crowd . . . I was a little overwhelmed."[24]

In the end, she was glad she had not taken the media criticism personally. "Any actress . . . cast would've gone through the same thing. But her fans were great once they saw me perform . . . In general, I think the Latin community is pretty happy that the project was made with a Latin writer-director, a Latin actress and an all-Latin cast and crew."[25]

Although the film was intended to be an objective retelling of Selena's life, it was Nava's intention for the film to be uplifting and not grief-filled. If there was a key to the performance for Jennifer, it was that she couldn't play the part with tragedy in mind. "One of the things I had to be careful of was that Selena never knew she was going to die," Jennifer points out. "I had to approach it in a very *alive* sense. The way I portrayed her was very, very true to the way she was. She was a jokester."[26]

One aspect of Selena's life Gregory Nava made a conscious choice to avoid was her death. The character of Yolanda Saldivar, the woman who shot Selena, is introduced later in the film and has little screen time. Instead of recreating the shooting, Nava uses the cinematic device of having a radio announcer explain what's happened while the audience sees Selena being rushed into an ambulance.

"I didn't want to make the movie about Yolanda, I wanted to make the movie about Selena," explains Nava. "The psychology of the person who pulls the trigger doesn't interest me. We're always in the head of the person who pulls the trigger. We have to start focusing on the victims of these violent actions. I wanted the last image of the movie to be Selena."[27]

Because of the similarities of their backgrounds and careers, occasionally Jennifer pondered the whimsy of fate. Celebrities have no choice but to watch their backs on a daily basis. Jennifer admits her managers frequently issue reminders about safety but Jennifer says you can only be so careful. The irony of Selena is that it wasn't a crazed stalker who took her life but someone from her innermost circle, proving to Jennifer that you've just got to live your life. For Jennifer, that meant concentrating on the job at hand, despite the controversies it continued to generate.

In the two years following her murder, it seemed as if the public had an insatiable desire to know every bit of minutia about Selena. But the filmmakers worried over whether that interest would still be there by the time the movie was released. Of even more concern to those involved with the film was the 1997 book by Maria Celeste Arraras, called *Selena's Secret: The Revealing Story Behind Her Tragic Death*. In the book, Arraras said

Selena's marriage to Pérez had been on the rocks at the time of her death; she was ready to leave her singing career behind to concentrate on her fashion empire; and Selena was romantically involved with the prominent Mexican plastic surgeon she had seen for liposuction treatments.

Naturally, in the press the family denied everything as shameless lies. Privately, though, some people close to Selena acknowledged the book was closer to the truth than Abraham would ever want revealed, lest Selena's golden image be tarnished. It began to seem as if the focus was shifting away from the film and Jennifer's dazzling performance in it, to a discussion about Abraham's control issues. But as the March 21 release date neared, Jennifer's star-making turn as Selena generated major buzz about being an Oscar-worthy performance. So as she had her entire career, Jennifer was once again involved in a project that continued to further the appreciation for, and advancement of, the Latino community. While Jennifer had never intended to be an activist or crusader, she knew her quickly rising celebrity profile was breaking all the old rules and took her position as trailblazer seriously. At the same time, she thought her million-dollar history-breaking salary for *Selena* said more about the industry than her. "It's a weird thing, because I know so many more people who make so much more money than me that it's kind of pathetic that I'm the highest-paid Latina actress. I just feel like Latinos have been underpaid in every way long enough. So I'm happy if I can help further the community in any way."[28]

But sometimes, as Jennifer would find out, it's impossible to please everybody. So when you're in a position where a lot of people want a piece of you, you're bound to always be disappointing somebody somewhere. Jennifer's first experience with being in the eye of an unexpected storm happened when plans for *Selena*'s premiere left many in the Hispanic community feeling hurt and betrayed.

Premieres are usually held in New York or Los Angeles although sometimes there are premieres held in both cities. They are usually invitation-only events where studio executives mingle with the film's actors, writers, and other members of the creative community. After the movie screens, there's a big party where everyone either toasts each other in celebration out of happiness at the movie's reception, or drowns their sorrows if the film is greeted with tepid interest. It has been this way in Hollywood for almost as long as there have been movies.

So nobody at the studio gave much thought of changing the status quo for *Selena*. However, because of Jennifer's work schedule, the premiere was scheduled to be in Miami where she was working on location. When Selena's ardent fans in her home state of Texas discovered they were being shut out of the festivities in favor of Florida, they felt forgotten and were upset.

Filmmakers are always sensitive to the mood of prospective ticket buyers and when the *Selena* brain trust got wind of the unhappy rumblings from Texas, they went into immediate damage control mode. Nancy De Los Santos, of Selena Film Productions, announced that due to overwhelming response and anticipation by fans, a total of 13 cities around the country would host gala screenings, including one in Selena's adopted home town of Corpus Christi, Texas, as well as one in San Antonio, home base of the singer's fan club.

It's tough enough to reassemble a cast, many of who are off working on other projects, for one screening but all the *Selena* actors were asked to four of the events—Washington D.C., Los Angeles, Corpus Christi, and San Antonio. Then selected actors would appear at the other venues based on availability. Although Washington D.C. was hardly a hotbed of Tejano music, the filmmakers hoped to inject a little politics into the proceedings on behalf of the Latino community and also hoped President Clinton would attend, which he did.

At the Corpus Christi screening, Jennifer was greeted by two thousand fans. And if there was one thing Jennifer says she learned from Selena was that it was important to treat fans like they mattered. "She was always very gracious, and always took time to talk to them," Jennifer says. "She realized that her fans were the most important things. There were a lot of ad-libs in the movie, and one of them was at the Grammy speech when she thanks her fans. It did happen in real life, but that wasn't in the script. I made sure to end the speech with a thank you to her fans. It was a constant thing with her from the time she won her first Tejano music award."[29]

In Corpus Christi, Jennifer addressed the crowd, admitting it was "hard to be somebody else, somebody who is so beloved. Selena meant a lot of different things to a lot of different people, and I had to do a good job for her fans. I think we pulled it off. By the end of filming, I could look in the mirror and really see her."[30] The question was: would fans and critics see the same reflection?

The eventual results were mixed. Overall, Jennifer was singled out for a dazzling performance, while the film itself was taken to task for the sense it had indeed presented a sugarcoated depiction of Selena's life and family. Jack Matthews of *Newsday* wrote, "I had the feeling that Nava had put the untouchable elements out of his mind and simply concentrated on what he could do, which was tap into the childlike joy that Selena got from her music and from performing . . . If you accept Abraham as approved by Abraham, the moments with the family resemble a Mexican-American *Father Knows Best*." He also praised "the brilliance of Lopez' performance."[31]

Chris Vognar, a writer for *The Dallas Morning News*, observed that "*Selena* skips over the teen years . . . Not to worry; the fast-forward brings us directly to the luminous Jennifer Lopez, a vulnerable powerhouse as the adult Selena. Selena's legend is still quite fresh, and Ms. Lopez is up to the daunting task of bringing her back to life. She doesn't disappoint, playing the budding star as a humbly dynamic figure capable of charming anyone."[32]

Of course some critics carry more weight than others, and Roger Ebert was one of those few critics that could sway people to see a film they otherwise might not. While he liked the film, he liked Jennifer more. "Lopez . . . has the star presence to look believable in front of 100,000 fans in Monterrey, Mexico . . . the results are electrifying . . . This is the kind of performance that can make a career."[33]

Jennifer took the comments in stride; she appreciated being complimented on her sensual appearance and didn't worry she was being pigeonholed as a result. "Latinas are sexy in general, but I'm not worried about stereotypes . . . sexy is not all that I am."[34]

Somewhere between the beginning of production and the release of the film, Jennifer had become one of Hollywood's new generation of bona fide movie stars, as well as an icon to the Latino community. While most actors with blossoming careers only have to worry about their own image and how it affected their careers, Jennifer seemed to be carrying the weight of an entire culture on her shoulders. But she saw it as an honor. "I feel like there's a pride in the Latin community about the fact that I'm out there. My voice teacher told me he has a few Latino girls that come to him and say, 'We're so proud of her.' That's a beautiful thing for me."[35]

The avalanche of discussion generated by *Selena* about Latinos in film was good for the Hispanic community but potentially detrimental to Jennifer—being held up as the new Latina icon could stereotype her in a way she had successfully avoided up to that point in her career. While she was fiercely proud of her heritage, she didn't want to be defined or limited by it. Jennifer wanted to be thought of as an actress, pure and simple.

The truth of the Hollywood matter was, the movies have always promoted stereotypes of all kinds. It's not so much that Hollywood had ignored Latinas, as much as they kept them assigned to a specific casting box. Some of the cinema's most glamorous screen sirens have been Hispanic. Back in the 1920s, Delores Del Rio first broke the color barrier and was cast in a number of films with South Pacific settings. Then Lupe Vélez ushered in the "spitfire." Then for a while, it seemed as if the path to stardom lay in trying to *become* the mainstream rather than trying to fit into the mainstream. Rita Hayworth in the 1940s and Raquel Welch in the 1970s cosmetically downplayed their ethnicity and achieved respectable success in return. But for today's generation of Latino stars it would be unthinkable to hide their heritage.

Certainly Jennifer didn't. Professionally, she was nobody's ethnic victim and nobody's creative doormat and was firmly in control of her career. "When I look to the future," she said in November 1996, "I don't see the pinnacle of what I'll reach, I see this endless hallway."[36]

Personally, however, she was about to discover that romance wasn't necessarily happily ever after the way it was in the movies.

NOTES

1. Julian Ives. Mr. *Showbiz*, 1997. http://www.lovelylopez.net/mrshowbiz interview.php

2. Ibid.

3. Henri Béhar. "On Selena." *Film Scouts*. http://www.filmscouts.com/ SCRIPTs/interview.cfm?File=jen-lop.

4. Ibid.

5. Julian Ives. Mr. *Showbiz*, 1997. http://www.lovelylopez.net/mrshowbiz interview.php.

6. Jeffrey Ressner. "Born To Play the Tejano Queen." *Time International*, March 24, 1997, p. 43.

7. *Selena* press kit for media. March, 1997.

8. Luaine Lee. "Olmos cleared a path for Hispanics." *Minneapolis Star Tribune*, May 17, 1997, p. 04E.

9. Ibid.

10. Bob Strauss. "How a former Fly Girl tackles Selena's memories, Oliver Stone's lunacy and (eeew!) giant killer snakes!" *Entertainment Online*, October 1996.

11. "The Making of Selena." *Hispanic*, March 31, 1997, p. PG.

12. Bob Strauss. "How a former Fly Girl tackles Selena's memories, Oliver Stone's lunacy and (eeew!) giant killer snakes!" *Entertainment Online*, October 1996.

13. Therese Poletti. "Reuters/Variety Entertainment Summary." *Reuters*, December 8, 1996.

14. Eric Guitierrez. "Busting Boundaries." *Newsday*, 16, 1997, p. C08.

15. Richard Corliss. "¡Viva Selena! The Queen Of Tejano Was Murdered In 1995. Now Hollywood And Her Father Present Their Version Of Her Life." *Time*, March 24, 1997, p. 86.

16. Julian Ives. Mr. *Showbiz*, 1997. http://www.lovelylopez.net/mrshowbiz interview.php.

17. Henri Béhar. "On Selena." *Film Scouts*. http://www.filmscouts.com/ SCRIPTs/interview.cfm?File=jen-lop.

18. Ibid.

19. Hillary Johnson. "Beauty Talk: Jennifer Lopez Star Of Selena." *In Style*, April 1, 1997, p. 91+.

20. Julian Ives. *Mr. Showbiz*, 1997. http://www.lovelylopez.net/mrshowbiz interview.php.

21. Bruce Westbrook. "'Selena' actress is on star track." *The Dallas Morning News*, August 2, 1996, p. 2C.

22. Ibid.

23. Dave Karger. "Biopicked for Stardom." *Entertainment Weekly*, August 9, 1996.

24. Bob Strauss. "Blood and Guts." *Chicago Sun-Times*, February 16, 1997. http://www.highbeam.com/doc/1P2-4374767.html.

25. Bruce Westbrook. "'Selena' actress is on star track." *The Dallas Morning News*, August 2, 1996, p. 2C.

26. Julian Ives. *Mr. Showbiz*, 1997. http://www.lovelylopez.net/mrshowbiz interview.php.

27. Mario Tarradell. "Selena's Power: Cultural Fusion." *The Dallas Morning News*, March 16, 1997, p. 1C.

28. Bob Strauss. "How a former Fly Girl tackles Selena's memories, Oliver Stone's lunacy and (eeew!) giant killer snakes!" *Entertainment Online*, October 1996.

29. Julian Ives. *Mr. Showbiz*, 1997. http://www.lovelylopez.net/mrshowbiz interview.php.

30. Richard Corliss. "¡Viva Selena! The Queen Of Tejano Was Murdered In 1995. Now Hollywood And Her Father Present Their Version Of Her Life." *Time*, March 24, 1997, p. 86.

31. Jack Mathews. "Though Muted by Dad, 'Selena' Sings." *Newsday*, March 21, 1997, p. B09.

32. Chris Vognar. "Selena: Biopic set firmly in ode mode." *The Dallas Morning News*, March 21, 1997, p. 1C.

33. Roger Ebert. "Lopez a convincing 'Selena'." *Minneapolis Star Tribune*, March 21, 1997, p. 06E.

34. Virginia Rohan. "The Spirit of Selena." *The Record* (Bergen County, NJ), March 20, 1997, p. y01.

35. Ibid.

36. "30 Under 30." *People* November 18, 1996. Available at http://www.people. com/people/archive/article/0,,20142784,00.html.

Jennifer's portrayal of doomed Tejano sensation Selena made her one of Hollywood's most sought after actresses and her million-dollar salary made her the highest paid Latina in film history. Warner Bros./Photofest.

Jennifer arrived at the 2000 Grammy ceremony with Sean "Puffy" Combs, wearing one of the most talked about dresses in Grammy history. She didn't realize it would cause such a stir saying, "I just thought it was a beautiful dress." Courtesy AP Photo/ Reed Saxon.

Jennifer feeds second husband, Chris Judd, some cake during their honeymoon in Italy at a party thrown by designer Donatella Versace. Courtesy AP Photo/Luca Bruno.

Jennifer's very public engagement to Ben Affleck ended abruptly when the wedding was called off days prior to the planned ceremony. Their careers didn't fare much better with the release of the critically panned Gigli, which bombed at the box office. Courtesy of Columbia Pictures/Photofest.

After her marriage to Marc Anthony, Jennifer kept a low public profile but branched out professionally as a producer. In 2006 she produced and costarred with Anthony in the film El Cantante. *Courtesy of Picture-house/Photofest.*

A very pregnant Jennifer and husband Marc Anthony arrive at Madonna's Gucci Benefit on February 6, 2008. Jennifer's pregnancy became one of Hollywood's best kept secrets; the couple did not acknowledge she was expecting until November 2007. *Courtesy AP Photo/Agostini.*

Chapter 7

BONA FIDE MOVIE STAR

Even if *Selena* hadn't been such a watershed role for Jennifer, she would always remember the production for a more personal reason. While filming on location in Texas, Jennifer's boyfriend, Ojani Noa, frequently joined her and was on hand for the wrap party after filming ended in late October 1996. Wrap parties tend to be emotional get-togethers. Not only is there a sense of relief at having finished the movie, but there's a sadness in knowing the temporary production family will be disbanding. In the case of the *Selena* wrap party, there was also the tacit awareness that the woman whose life they had celebrated on film wasn't around anymore.

But even so, the mood was festive at the Hard Rock Cafe in San Antonio where the cast and crew drank margaritas and danced to salsa music, with Jennifer showing off her dance moves with Ojani. When she finally took a breather, Ojani grabbed a microphone and walked up to a bemused Jennifer, who thought her boyfriend was going to say something about her work in the movie. Instead, Noa proposed to her—in Spanish.

Jennifer was so shocked she burst into tears. A few of the more cautious-minded in the crowd yelled out that perhaps Jennifer should think it over a moment but Jennifer had already said yes. "Then he gets down on one knee and puts the ring on my finger. It was very, very romantic."[1]

Jennifer says the reason she didn't have to think about it was because she already had. She also admits it wasn't a question of whether or not she'd say yes, only where and when Ojani would pop the question. So confident was Noa that when they got back from the wrap party, "He picks up the calendar and goes, 'We're getting married on such and such date.' That was that."[2]

On one level, it was easy to imagine Jennifer and Ojani as the happy couple. She claims she had always gone for Latino guys and Ojani had classic dark good looks that had led to some modeling. Ojani also had some designs on acting as well, although Jennifer sounded skeptical. "I'm like, 'After you've seen what I've been through, working nonstop these past six months, you want to be an actor? You retard!' But I don't know, I guess I make it look easy."[3]

When Jennifer came back to the Bronx for a Christmas visit, she also brought along a brand-new black, four-door Cadillac for her mother. It was important for Jennifer to include her friends and family in her success, in part because she loved them deeply but also because she never wanted to forget her roots—something that was equally important to her mom, who says that while Jennifer may be living in Los Angeles, her heart would always be in the Bronx.

Her apartment may have been in Los Angeles and her heart in the Bronx, but Jennifer herself was seldom in either place. Her next film was *U-Turn*. When Jennifer auditioned for director Oliver Stone in early 1996, the Oscar-winning filmmaker was immediately taken with her. For Jennifer, the irony about working with Stone was that earlier in her career, she had a disastrous audition with him that left her thoroughly insulted. Stone had been casting for a project about former Panamanian dictator Manuel Noriega. In the middle of her audition, Stone began walking around the room and rearranging the furniture. Jennifer was stunned at his rude behavior and says Stone continued moving around furniture until she finished her reading. Afterward, according to a February 1998 interview she gave in *Movieline* magazine, she immediately called her manager and told him she had never been treated so shabbily and that she would *never* work for Oliver Stone.

But in Hollywood *never* seldom means never. It's the nature of the business that people's paths cross at the most unexpected times for the most unexpected projects. Plus, someone who's on top of the movie world and an arrogant dilettante one year can be the humbled artist looking to make both a comeback and amends the next. Or, they can be at the helm of a project an actor simply wants too badly to carry a grudge.

When Jennifer's agents called her about meeting with Stone for his new movie, she reminded them of her unwillingness to work with the man and got off the phone. But when she got back from filming *Anaconda*, the director had called again asking for her to come in and read. "I'm one of those people who usually sticks to something I've said," she says "but I got to thinking, 'Well, he called himself and he wants to make amends. I have the upper hand here because I don't care about this movie.

I've got Selena and I'm getting a million dollars for it.'"[4] Suddenly realizing she didn't *need* Stone made it okay for Jennifer to go in and see what would happen this time. She had just learned an important lesson on how powerful saying *no* could be. She also learned how important it was to be in the financial position to say no.

To Jennifer's surprise, she and Stone hit it off and she had a good time making the movie. *U-Turn* was a dark comedy. In the film, Jennifer plays an Apache Indian living in a small desert town with her husband. She becomes attracted to a down-on-his-luck gambler, played by Sean Penn, who is in deep debt to the Russian mob. When her husband catches them in a romantic embrace, he breaks the gambler's nose then offers him a business proposition—to kill his wife. Then the wife offers the stranger a proposition of her own—to kill her husband. The gambler, who desperately needs money to pay back the mob, has to decide which offer to take.

Jennifer admitted later that she became smitten with Penn during the filming.

"I was engaged when we were shooting *U-Turn*, and one day he said, 'If I weren't married and you weren't engaged, would this have been a very different movie?' And I go, 'Yeah! Very different.'" But, as Jennifer firmly added, "we both had our own lives, so that made a real difference."[5]

Despite their flirtation, Jennifer was never tempted to cheat on her fiancé. "No, because I'm a one-man woman. If I'm content in a relationship, I'm fine." However, she also revealed that perhaps Noa wasn't quite as at ease with certain aspects of her job, such as her cinematic love scenes with Sean Penn. "You know how Latin men are—very passionate. This is all new to us, so we're both kind of feeling our way through it. We have our rough times, but we love each other."[6]

For the Catholic-raised Jennifer, fidelity was an important issue, especially in a profession where the temptations can be powerful and daily. Although she believes in fidelity, she acknowledged you could still be attracted to someone other than the person you were in love with. She also said defining fidelity was difficult. "It's difficult to pinpoint exactly when someone is being unfaithful. To me, when you're sharing your life with someone and then you start having feelings for someone else, then that's infidelity. I'm faithful."[7]

At a point not too far in the future, those words would ring hollow in Ojani Noa's ears. But for then, their romance was in full bloom and all was right in their world, just as all was right in Jennifer's professional world. Although *U-Turn* was more of an art house favorite than a mainstream hit, it was greeted with mostly positive reviews.

While *U-Turn* had been an interesting professional excursion, Jennifer was relieved when it was over. She had been working non-stop for over a year, which left little if any time for a social life. At times she longed for time to just kick back. "I'm a regular girl," she said during one junket. "I like to shop, I like to go to the mall and hang out and get facials, get my nails done and buy shoes. And I've still got a lot of publicity to do over the next few months. Right now, just being at home sounds real nice."[8]

But she wasn't exactly being idle. Jennifer started to drop hints that she was looking to expand her professional résumé to include singer. The idea had begun percolating in her mind while filming *Selena*. Even though the producers used Selena's real recordings in the movie, during the concert Jennifer was actually singing. So the response from the crowd was real and reminded Jennifer just how much she enjoyed performing on stage in from of a live audience. "That week I told my managers that I want to record something," Jennifer recalled shortly after *Selena* wrapped. "I've gotta record an album. I love doing it so much. So maybe that's something to work on this year."[9]

But before she could embark on a fledgling music career, Jennifer, then 26, had other commitments to meet, such as getting married. She and Ojani had set the date for February 22, 1997, a little over a year since their first date. The ceremony was held at the home of Ojani's friend Joe Fernandez, an American Airlines flight attendant who had known Noa since he came to the United States on a raft from his native Cuba five years earlier.

With money not an issue, Jennifer had a wedding planner set up a parquet dance floor at Fernandez's home where the house band from Larios—Norberto and Marisela and the Caribbean Septet—would play. Jennifer flew in New York hairstylist Oscar Blandi and treated her mother and sister to a professional make-over. Her $500 bouquet had stephanotis, orchids, and crystalline roses. Downstairs Ojani waited nervously, looking movie star handsome in his velvet Versace tuxedo. The bride-to-be had chosen an ivory Escada dress with a lace train. Off-duty police officers patrolled the property's perimeter in order to thwart any paparazzi that might be lurking about.

After a brief half-hour meet-and-mingle, the Catholic ceremony began at three in the afternoon and was attended by two hundred of their family and friends. Guards be damned, determined paparazzi were seen climbing nearby streetlights, hoping to get a photo of the happy couple. The service was conducted in both Spanish and English. When the bride walked out of the house on the arm of her father, Ojani reportedly burst into tears. Later, as Jennifer danced with her dad David, Abraham Quintanilla openly wept.

But no amount of tears could dampen the day's festivities. And Jennifer made sure everyone got into a celebratory mood. She had the band play a merengue and pulled *Selena* co-star Edward James Olmos to his feet and the two of them showed off their impeccable dance moves to the delight of the onlookers. Characterized by swiveling hips and a sinuous rib cage, merengue and salsa dancing is incredibly sensual when done well. The man leads, but the focus is on the woman, who provides most of the movement via turns and dips. Following the bride's lead, as it were, Jennifer and Ojani's guests danced late into the night and were still partying when the newlyweds said their goodbyes. The couple spent a weeklong honeymoon in Key West, Florida, spending most of the days just sitting on the beach relaxing.

ACTION HEROINE

After her brief honeymoon with Ojani, Jennifer was back at work. And this time out, she was back toting a gun. But unlike her experience in *Money Train*, where she played second fiddle to the antics of Woody Harrelson and Wesley Snipes, in *Out of Sight* she was the leading lady opposite George Clooney, who was a Hollywood sensation in his own right. Jennifer joked that is was a nice change to have her co-star be the sex symbol in the movie.

Clooney had been knocking around Hollywood for a decade before he landed the role of Dr. Doug Ross on the television ratings phenomenon, *ER*. His down-to-earth personality and his dark, brooding good looks made him an overnight heartthrob and it wasn't long before movie producers came pounding on his door. But as many television actors have learned, making the transition from the small screen to film stardom can be fraught with peril. *Out of Sight* would be Clooney's fifth film and up to that point, his box office record was spotty at best. Some would even say disappointing, with his stint as Batman in *Batman and Robin* being the most disappointing of them all.

With typical self-deprecation, he joked, "I think I buried the franchise," then added more seriously, "The outcome of *Batman* ultimately was disappointing. I don't mean just box-office-wise; I mean as a film. I take responsibility for some of that; I'm playing Batman, so I have got to take some heat for that . . . It ended up making money for the studio. The problem is that the studio is used to making so much money that it can carry them for other bad films or whatever through the summer, and this one didn't do that for them.[10]

"Now that I've gone through the great-break period—*Batman* was the greatest break of my career—now it's about choices," Clooney said. "This is the first one that's just my choice. This time I'm not wearing any rubber suit, which I think will be the key."[11]

Clooney suspected his problem in finding the role that would jump start his film career was that he was down on the Hollywood pecking order when it came to being offered roles. "I don't know this for a fact, but I'm sure that some of the big guys passed on it along the way," Clooney mused about the role in *Out of Sight*. "I'm on that list where about four or five people have to go, 'Nah, I'm too busy.' Then I get it."[12]

Unlike Jennifer, Clooney didn't exude a burning ambition and joked that he imagined a day when his popularity would wane and life would settle into a calm and sedate daily rhythm. His attitude was, "If you want to see me on TV or in a movie, you do that. And when you don't, I will go away—which I will eventually. There are very few Paul Newmans in the world. I'm doing dinner theater in about ten years. In the end, I'm going to end up on Hollywood Squares."[13]

Because Clooney had already gone through what Jennifer was just beginning to experience—the intense and occasionally uncomfortable glare of media interest—he could offer some hard-earned and sage advice about the pressures of celebrity and how to cope. "It's weird," he says, "the work you have to do to stay somewhat normal. Not a day goes by—literally not a day—that there isn't some story about me in some newspaper that's completely wrong. I read I was at Cindy Crawford's wedding, sitting on the beach talking to Richard Gere. I'm reading this in New York, thinking, *Wow! Was I there?*"[14]

That said, Clooney thinks its wasted energy, and maybe just *this much* disingenuous to get upset. "I don't like actors complaining how miserable their life is," he says. "I'm very well paid and I love what I do. But if you spend a day walking around with me, you'd rethink whether you want to be me. You can be walking through an airport and here comes some 17-year-old with a video camera, and he starts making fun of your female assistant to get a response. He wants me to go, 'Screw you,' and shove him, and that's the clip they'll play over and over."[15]

To get the role of Federal Agent Karen Sisco, Jennifer Lopez had to beat out Sandra Bullock. She auditioned with Clooney, reading a scene that has their two characters locked in a car trunk together. "George and I were in this office and we laid down together on a couch," recalls Jennifer. "We did the trunk scene and when we finished, I think I got it. I'll do that kind of stuff to get parts."[16]

And once she gets the roles, she works hard to prepare. Since she was playing a federal marshal, Jennifer decided to spend some time with real female law enforcement officers. "You learn more by observing people than by asking questions so I tagged along with these tough-guy cops and just observed—like when a female cop is standing with a male cop, people talk to the male cop. So women find ways to demand respect. They don't let men one-up them in anything. They banter with them line for line. They shoot with them shot for shot."[17]

One thing Clooney and Jennifer had in common besides their sex symbol status was their mutual fatigue. While Jennifer had been working on back-to-back-to-back-to-back films for almost two years, Clooney was doing double duty, flying back and forth between the *Out of Sight* locations and Los Angeles, where *ER* was in production. During the filming, Jennifer and Clooney shared an easy rapport and teased each other about their status as movie stars.

Out of Sight was the first film that translated the charisma that had made him so popular on *ER* onto the large screen. In the movie, Clooney plays Jack Foley, a charming, if not particularly successful, career bank robber who holds up banks but never carries a weapon. The movie opens with Foley robbing a bank in Florida. After leaving the bank, he unhurriedly gets into his car only to discover it won't start, making a getaway impossible. Cut to Foley breaking out of jail with the help of his friend Buddy, a hapless criminal who has an unfortunate tendency to confess his crimes to his sister, a nun, who then promptly turns her brother in. Just as Foley is breaking out of jail, his escape is witnessed by federal marshal Karen Sisco. So Buddy stuffs her into his car trunk, where Jack is also hidden.

The movie hinges on making the audience believe that a federal agent could find herself both attracted to and falling for a bank robber. "Every movie asks you to take one thing and just accept it," Clooney says. "I'm going to have to believe that a meteor is going to hit the Earth. Or I have to believe that the lizard is going to walk through New York. You *have* to, or it doesn't work. For this one, it's that a girl, in the time period that we're in a trunk together, is able to at least be open to the idea of falling in love with the guy who's holding her hostage. That's a trick. It wasn't a trick for my character because I'm breaking out of jail and met a nice girl. That's easy for me. It was much tougher for Jennifer. She had all the acting work. We actually re-shot it to get it just right," he says of the trunk scene. "I actually love it now."[18]

Plus, Karen's background isn't necessarily as conservative as her job suggests. She's involved in a tepid romance with a married FBI agent and she includes among her old boyfriends a bank robber. So even though Foley might not consciously know it, instinctively he realizes he has a chance to win Sisco's heart. Of course, Karen's law and order officer dad would have apoplexy if he knew.

After releasing Sisco, Foley heads for Detroit where he intends to stage one last robbery to net enough money so he can retire from crime. But everywhere Jake turns, Karen seems to be there and even though she could cost him his freedom, he can't seem to stay away from her. Nor does he want to.

The movie was directed by one-time Hollywood wunderkind Steven Soderbergh, who burst on the scene in 1989 with *sex, lies and videotape*. Just 26 at the time, Soderbergh's film won both the audience award at Sundance and the Palme d'Or at Cannes. Costing only $1.2 million to produce, the film earned $30 million at the box office.

But after that auspicious beginning, Soderbergh had struggled to duplicate his debut success, or even come close to it. Prior to 1998's *Out of Sight*, he had directed a string of poorly received, low grossing films. Soderbergh had fallen so far below the mainstream radar that many in the industry were surprised he got as plum an assignment as *Out of Sight*. Just as many people in the independent film world seemed surprised that Soderbergh would want to work on a studio-funded film.

Soderbergh has said he simply goes to whatever project seems the most engaging. "*Out of Sight*, like some of the others, just came up. Someone at Universal called and said, 'We've got a project here that needs a director and I really think this would be a good studio movie for you because I think you'll be able to do something with it. And what you will do with it will be in line with what we're thinking ought to be done with it.' And he was right. I've never gotten a piece of material from a studio before that I really felt that way about. I guess that's why it took so long because I was just instinctively waiting for the thing that I knew I could do."[19]

That kind of confidence was important, because with a big budget comes expectations. "I think that's why it was a little scary," Soderbergh admitted. "We had all the resources to make a good movie and if we didn't it was going to be embarrassing. You don't always feel that way. Normally, all your focus is on trying to fix stuff. This is the first time it felt like there really isn't anything to fix here. I just need to not . . . blow it. That's a different kind of thing."[20]

However, there were also some upsides with doing a studio picture. "It was really nice making a movie that I knew was coming out on such and such a date in so many theatres because I'd never done that before," Soderbergh pointed out. "I've never made a movie that had a release date before."[21]

Nor had he ever had to film anyone with quite so famous a behind as Jennifer. When asked at the premiere if he had to shoot her in any particular way because she looked so svelte in the film, Soderbergh shook his head. Jennifer heard the question and laughed. "If they get a butt shot," she said, "it's gonna be a wide one; that's just the bottom line!"[22]

The chemistry between Jennifer and Clooney gave the movie's pivotal love scene a crackling energy. But it wasn't a typical love scene. "We said, 'We can't just kiss and take off our clothes. What are we going to do?'" Jennifer recalls. "I started to take off my sweater and we figured, so let's do like a strip poker thing. You start taking off your tie and I take off an earring and he takes off his watch. It becomes a game and by the end the anticipation was too much."[23]

The sexual combustion that propelled that scene was evident throughout the film and to the surprise of many, *Out of Sight* became an unexpected hit, both with critics and at the box office when it was released in June 1998.

In a year-end review of cinema, *Entertainment Weekly* noted, "It's not like we have to convince you that getting locked in a trunk with George Clooney was a good thing for Jennifer Lopez. But *Out of Sight* may have been the best thing for both their careers: Her icy hot federal marshal, thrown together with Clooney's bank-robbing misfit, displayed charms beyond the obvious. And like a modern-day Ginger Rogers, the smoldering Jennifer finally made classy Clooney sexy on the big screen."[24]

Critic Owen Gleiberman saw the film as a turning point in Jennifer's career. "Lopez, for all her Latina-siren voluptuousness, has always projected a contained coolness, and this is the first movie in which it fully works for her. As Sisco is lured into a romance with Foley, you can see her resolve melt in spite of itself . . . *Out of Sight* is so light it barely stays with you, but it's more fun around the edges than most movies are at their centers."[25]

Minneapolis Star Tribune critic Colin Covert called the movie "a stylish, clever cops-and-crooks yarn with a hot romantic twist: The gorgeous fed and the macho bank robber have a thing for each other. George Clooney and Jennifer Lopez generate sparks in every scene together, and the film is flawlessly cast down to the smallest supporting role . . . It's rare that a movie gives us one likable, root-for-'em protagonist, let alone two. *Out of Sight* has you hoping that they'll both win. But, of course, they can't. Or can they? . . ."[26]

The Dallas Morning News, which had followed Jennifer's career closely since her role as Selena, announced, "With this film, Ms. Lopez also comes fully into her own. She sizzles as a tough woman with a human side. And she and Mr. Clooney share a chemistry that elevates their romance above the opposites-attract cliché. The supporting cast is also dynamic."[27]

In almost every review, the supporting actors in the film were repeatedly singled out for their performances—something that could dent the ego of certain leading men and women. But Jennifer and Clooney were just as supportive of the supporting players as they were each other. "The truth is you can't worry about that," Clooney said. "You just hope everybody does the best they can and they bring the whole project up. I think Steve Zahn steals the whole movie, and that's great. I get to be part of it."[28]

But this film was Clooney and Jennifer's star turn, earning them the best reviews yet of their respective careers. Janet Maslin of the *New York Times* wrote, "Ms. Lopez has her best movie role thus far, and she brings it both seductiveness and grit; if it was hard to imagine a hard-working, pistol-packing bombshell on the page, it couldn't be easier here."[29]

Out of Sight cemented Jennifer's bankability. However, just as her star was rising, so was her reputation for being a difficult leading lady—and occasional loose fashion cannon.

NOTES

1. Dennis Hensley. "How do you say 'hot' in Spanish?" *Cosmopolitan 222*, April 1, 1997, p. 190.

2. Ibid.

3. Bob Strauss. "How a former Fly Girl tackles Selena's memories, Oliver Stone's lunacy and (eeew!) giant killer snakes!" *Entertainment Online*, October 1996.

4. Stephen Rebello. "The Wow." *Movieline*, February 1998. http://members. aol.com/dafreshprinz/jenniferlopez/movieline0298.htm.

5. Ibid.

6. Dennis Hensley. "How do you say 'hot' in Spanish?" *Cosmopolitan 222*, April 1, 1997, p. 190.

7. Anthony Noguera. *FHM*, December 1998. http://www.beyond-beautiful. org/topic/412/t/FHM-December-1998.html.

8. Beyond Beautiful.com. http://www.beyond-beautiful.org/topic/783/t/Jen-Interview.html.

9. Julian Ives. *Mr. Showbiz*, 1997. http://www.lovelylopez.net/mrshowbiz interview.php.

10. Philip Wuntch. "Clooney tunes up his career with new film." *The Dallas Morning News*, June 26, 1998, p. 7.

11. Margaret A. McGurk. "This role is one Clooney really wanted." *Cincinnati Enquirer*, June 30, 1998, p. ARC.

12. "Clooney scores directing hit." *BBC News*. December 23, 2002. http:// news.bbc.co.uk/1/low/entertainment/film/2600935.stm.

13. Ibid.

14. John Powers and Terry Gross. "'Out of Sight.'" *Fresh Air* (NPR), July 10, 1998.

15. Ibid.

16. Patricia Duncan. *Jennifer Lopez*. New York: Macmillan, 1999.

17. Jeffrey Zaslow. "Straight Talk." *USA Today Weekend*, June 19–21, 1998. http://www.usaweekend.com/98_issues/980621/980621talk_lopez.html.

18. Margaret A. McGurk. "This role is one Clooney really wanted." *Cincinnati Enquirer*, June 30, 1998, p. ARC.

19. "Names in the News." *AP Online*, June 22, 1998.

20. Marjorie Baumgarten. "Nine Year Itch." *Austin Chronicle*, June 29, 1998.

21. Ibid.

22. "Jennifer Lopez: She's proud of her 'bottom line.'" *USA Today*, July 2, 1998, p. 14D.

23. Stephen Schaefer. "Plenty of Clooney in view in 'Out of Sight' love scene." *USA Today*, June 12, 1998, p. 03E.

24. Owen Gleiberman. "It Takes a Thief." *Entertainment Weekly*, June 26, 1998, p. 100+.

25. Ibid.

26. Colin Covert. "'Out of Sight' is one worth seeing." *Minneapolis Star Tribune*, June 26, 1998, p. 15E.

27. Philip Wuntch. "Clooney tunes up his career with new film." *The Dallas Morning News*, June 26, 1998, p. 7.

28. Margaret A. McGurk. "This role is one Clooney really wanted." *Cincinnati Enquirer*, June 30, 1998, p. ARC.

29. Janet Maslin. *The New York Times*, June 4, 1998. http://query.nytimes.com/gst/fullpage.html?res=9B05E5DB103AF935A15755C0A96E958260.

Chapter 8

TOUGH LESSONS

In March 1997, Jennifer Lopez attended her first Academy Awards ceremony with her husband of one month in tow. Relatively speaking, Jennifer was sedately dressed but it would be one of the last awards nights where her outfit would go unnoticed. Afterwards, she and Ojani headed for Morton's restaurant, where *Vanity Fair* was hosting its annual post-Oscar bash. Invitations to this affair are among the most coveted in Hollywood. Among the guests were Jim Carrey, director Quentin Tarantino, Tom Cruise, Nicole Kidman, and Ellen DeGeneres, who would, that very night, meet Anne Heche. Their subsequent relationship eventually led DeGeneres to come out publicly.

In May, *People* magazine named Jennifer one of its 50 Most Beautiful People in the World. Interviewed for her profile, Jennifer talked about how she enjoyed accentuating her curvy body. She also maintained that her growing celebrity put a damper on some of her self-pampering activities, such as going to a spa for a massage. "I can't be naked in public," she said, because "I would read in the tabloids about how I have a mole on my back!"[1]

But what Jennifer was actually reading in the tabloids was quite a bit more distressing than reports of skin imperfections. In May 1997, just three months after her glamorous wedding, reports surfaced that her marriage to Noa was as good as over. Speculation began after the two had a loud dispute in a Los Angeles restaurant that ended when Noa stomped out. Jennifer's publicist issued a vehement denial, claiming that the couple was still madly in love and that Jennifer had never been happier. In fact, the publicist revealed that the lovebirds had just given themselves a second wedding, this time in Malibu, which was attended by Jennifer's friends from the Hollywood community.

That November, entertainment editors and writers were sent a clip from Puff Daddy's new music video for "Been around the World." According to the accompanying press release, "The epic tale takes our hero (Puffy) from a suburban home to the desert of a nondescript Middle Eastern country . . ."[2] Once there, he protects "the beautiful princess," played by Jennifer. Featured throughout this so-called video epic were limousines and private jets; there were also some exquisite ballroom scenes and a surprise dance sequence performed by Jennifer Lopez and Puff Daddy.

The release went on to cite Puffy's musical achievements, including the fact that his album *No Way Out* debuted at number one on Billboard's "Top 200 Albums" and "Top R&B Albums" charts, and that he had held the number-one position on Billboard's "Hot Rap Singles" chart for 42 consecutive weeks. What the release didn't say was that while still in his twenties, Combs had become one of the top rap moguls in the music business, controlling an empire worth an estimated $250 million. He amassed his fortune by making hip-hop safe for mainstream America, with the help of such artists as Mary J. Blige, Jodeci, and the Notorious B.I.G. His own album, *No Way Out*, sold in excess of six million copies.

Nor was Puffy shy about flaunting his success. He drove a $375,000 powder-blue Bentley and owned a $2.5 million estate in Easthampton, New York. His guests included gangsta rappers as well as Donald Trump and Martha Stewart. He was everything Ojani Noa wasn't—professionally successful, driven, and Jennifer's creative and financial peer. It's not difficult to understand why she would turn to someone like Puff Daddy when she needed a confidante. And, in the beginning, the two insisted that friendship was all their relationship was about.

But Jennifer and Ojani were living increasingly separate lives. Jennifer traveled solo to work and public appearances while Noa busied himself with his new job as manager of the Conga Room, a Los Angeles club that Jennifer had invested in. At the Conga Room Noa could meet and greet the top names in Latin music as well as rub elbows with celebrities. The celebrity he was married to, however, was preparing to live apart from him. It seemed as though she was sounding the death knell of their union when she commented, "It's tough for me because the men I'm attracted to, for some reason, haven't gotten it together . . . Ojani is never gonna make as much money as me."[3]

Jennifer was asked to be a presenter at the March 1998 Oscars and again, she showed up without Ojani. Jennifer reveled in the perks bestowed upon her for appearing on the awards telecast; she got to take home a pile of lavish gifts, including a Baccarat crystal pendant, a bottle of Bulgari fragrance, a gift certificate for Frederic Fekkai's Beaute de Provence Day, a Harry Winston sterling silver compass, a JBL stereo CD system, a Montblanc Wolfgang Amadeus Mozart pen, a bottle of Mumm's Cordon Rouge champagne, a Steiff teddy bear, and a Tag Heuer watch. Several papers reported that later at the Miramax post-Oscar party, Jennifer and Puffy got extremely cozy.

That same month, Sony Music's Work Group announced it had signed an exclusive, long-term recording deal with Jennifer Lopez. "It was a no-brainer," Work Group's co-president Jeff Ayeroff told *Entertainment Weekly*. "I was like, 'I'm a fish. You're a hook.'"[4] Sony Music Entertainment president and chief operating officer Tommy Mottola, who had recently split from his onetime protégée-turned-wife Mariah Carey, said in a press statement, "As great an actress as she is, Jennifer Lopez is also a gifted musical performer. Jennifer is going to surprise a lot of people who have never glimpsed this facet of her artistry."[5] In a less guarded moment, Mottola said, "I listened to it and called her. She's not Aretha Franklin, but who is?"[6]

After the announcement, Jennifer turned to Puffy even more, and the music impresario agreed to write a cut for the album she was planning. By May 1998, it had become obvious that their relationship had passed beyond the level of professional friendship. Late in the month, the *New York Post* broke the story that their rumored romance was a fact. According to the paper's "Page Six" section, Jennifer and Combs had spent "two steamy days—and nights" at a hotel in Miami's South Beach.[7] They'd been observed by other guests frolicking around the pool, and Jennifer was staying in Puffy's luxury penthouse.

Elsewhere it was reported that Combs had hotel security on patrol to make sure nobody snapped any pictures of them. The news was doubly surprising to fans of Combs and Jennifer. Jennifer, of course, was believed to be married; and Puffy had long been involved with Kim Porter, who had just given birth to their son in April. But the *Post* article indicated that Jennifer's romance with Puffy was an open secret within music-industry circles and that neither seemed particularly interested in hiding their affection for one another.

Jennifer's representatives immediately issued a denial, calling the allegations completely untrue, maintaining the pair were just good friends. Asked why Jennifer was with Puffy in Miami in the first place, they explained that she was in town shooting a movie. A month later in June 1998, all these denials were revealed to have been nothing more than spin control. On *Good Morning America*, gossip columnist Cindy Adams reported that she had spoken in person to Ojani Noa, and Noa had told her that he and Jennifer had indeed split up. But Noa denied that it was Puffy who had stolen Jennifer away, claiming instead that the breakup was because of her career.[8]

In another wire report, Ojani announced that he and Jennifer had been separated since the beginning of 1998 and had divorced in March. "She wanted the divorce," he said. "She also gave me money and paid for my lawyer. She wanted her career so everything with us went out the window. People change . . . I'm in pain. I loved her a lot."[9]

Gossip columnist Cindy Adams also suggested that Jennifer's butt had been resculpted: "It's just that she had what she used to call a very well-developed booty, and since I am not exactly derriere-impaired my-self, I don't like to say too much, but when she stood sideways, it looked like a Dodge hatchback."[10]

Jennifer herself insisted that she was simply getting into better over-all shape. Prior to filming *Out of Sight*, she had hired two trainers who whipped her into even better shape through a regimen of weights, boxing, and water aerobics. Jennifer also went on a high-protein, low-fat diet. And Jennifer seemed intent on showing off her toned body whenever pos-sible. At the MTV Movie Awards in June, she wore a relatively demure leather skirt with a very revealing Paco Rabanne halter top, which one reporter referred to as a "metallic halter-cum-napkin."[11]

After the award ceremonies, over one thousand guests were escorted to the post-show party tent. An array of semi-clad female celebrities pa-raded in, including among them Denise Richards, Jennifer Love Hewitt, Carmen Electra, and Courtney Cox. Not everyone approved. Vivica A. Fox, dressed in a tasteful pantsuit, told *People* magazine, "I just want to go up to these girls and say, 'Honey, put your bra on!'" Others, of course, thought this display of near-nudity wasn't necessarily such a bad thing. "It's all about how much your body can handle," designer Marc Bouwer explained. "Because nobody wants to look at saggy boobs and wrinkled skin. But if you have a great body, why not show it?"[12]

Although Jennifer may have been a photographer's dream with her scanty outfits, she was starting to run afoul of some of her peers, who may have thought that she should perhaps wear a new accessory—a sock in her mouth. In the February 1997 issue of *Movieline*, Jennifer gave a very lengthy, very straight-from-the-hip interview to Stephen Rebello. In the course of their chat, she managed to diss a number of her peers and a few entertainment heavyweights.

At Rebello's prompting, Jennifer called Salma Hayek, who went on to produce the series *Ugly Betty*, "a sexy bombshell" stuck playing a certain kind of role while she herself could "do all kinds of different things." Jennifer also implied that Hayek was a liar because she claimed to have been offered the lead in *Selena*. Jennifer went on to explain that Columbia executives had given her the choice of *Anaconda* or the Matthew Perry vehicle *Fools Rush In*, and that Hayek had been given the latter only after Jennifer chose "the fun B-movie because the *Fools* script wasn't strong enough."[13]

Now on a roll Jennifer called Cameron Diaz a "lucky model." When asked about Gwyneth Paltrow, she asked back, "Tell me what she's been in? . . . I heard more about her and Brad Pitt than I ever heard about her work." She called her *U-Turn* co-star Claire Danes "a good actress," but added that Danes was starting to do "the same thing with every character she does."[14]

Then Jennifer said a few unflattering things about Jack Nicholson and Wesley Snipes, blasted her producers for underpaying her, and professed to be unable to understand why Winona Ryder was so "revered. I've never heard anyone in the public or among my friends say, 'Oh, I love her . . .'" Winding down, Jennifer said that she considered Madonna to be a "great performer" but that her acting skills left a lot to be desired. She also announced that she was tired of hearing people say acting is easy. "Acting is what I do, so I'm harder on people when they say, 'Oh, I can do that—I can act.' I'm like, 'Hey, don't spit on my craft.'"[15]

The fallout from this stream of critical commentary was immediate and predictable. Columnists everywhere took Jennifer to task, including some Latino journalists who had always supported her in the past. Angelo Figueroa, then-managing editor of *People en Espanol*, ran an item about the furor. "Her publicist called me and said, 'How could you do this to Jennifer Lopez? You're Latino, you're her own people?' I'm, like, 'I am not Jennifer's publicist, I am here to report the news. And if Jennifer Lopez decides to say that Jack Nicholson is a legend in his own mind . . . and that, you know, Gwyneth Paltrow can't act . . . she just really dissed a whole bunch of folks. If she says that, that's news.'"[16]

Some of Jennifer's directors tried to come to her aid. Steven Soderbergh announced that he would gladly work with her again, while Gregory Nava said that Jennifer was still mastering a steep learning curve. "It's impossible for people to imagine how overwhelming stardom can be. Everybody that this happens to has a period where they have to learn how to deal with it. Jennifer's very level-headed, and she's going to come through all of that with bells on."[17] Casting agent Roger Mussenden also lent a little support: "Jennifer Lopez is a ball buster—outspoken and strong. Some people may not look at that as positive, but I think it is strength in character."[18]

Jennifer tried to defuse the situation by sending letters of apology to those she had publicly insulted, but the damage had been done. Overnight, her image had been tarnished. Terms like *difficult, self-absorbed*, and *diva* started to be bandied about. Some studio flacks started complaining anonymously. One Universal publicist let it be known that nobody could ever be sure that Jennifer would show up where and when she was supposed to. She showed up an hour late for a *Today* interview. A *Newsweek* interview was scrapped after she canceled it three times. Then, in the summer of 1998, she and publicist Karynne Tencer severed their business relationship, and Jennifer was left without a personal mouthpiece. Despite her high profile, she reportedly found it very difficult to find a new publicist right away. Her reputation was undermining her. Putting on a brave face, she said, "Who cares? I don't. I'm just being who I am. I don't try to be nice. I don't try to be not nice."[19] Jennifer was well aware that she was now being called a diva—in the most derisive sense of the word. It was a term she took offense at because she felt "it means that you are mean to people, that you look down on people, and I'm not that type of person."[20]

Perhaps not, but her apparent lack of cooperation and the perception that she had been repeatedly caught telling lies to the media about her relationship with Puffy Combs had dimmed her once-golden glow. As late as October 1998, she was still publicly denying her romantic involvement with Combs. Her association with Combs did nothing to improve her standing within the Hollywood mainstream. Many thought that she was playing with fire. In an interview on *Good Morning America,* she responded to a question about her *Out of Sight* character that was obviously about Combs instead. "What is it about bad boys? I don't know, there's something just so attractive about them. I always say that it's like it's a protection thing. It's, like—it's exciting and fun, because it's dangerous. But also you feel like you're protected. It's, like, you know, little girls looking up to their dad, they feel safe. And there's something about a bad guy that you just feel safe with. I don't know why."[21]

Jennifer seemed to be thinking out loud, struggling to explain. Still supposedly speaking about *Out of Sight*, she added, "It's about when you're faced with one of those situations in your life where it just changes; you meet somebody, and it changes everything . . . And all of a sudden, you're battling, and you have this conflict . . . You're just rethinking all of the stuff that you've always gone by, all the morals and values you went by your whole life. All of a sudden, everything's just turned around and crazy."[22]

There was no denying Sean Combs had been spectacularly successful in building himself a career but the gangsta mystique that Puff Daddy, like so many other hip-hop and rap artists intentionally projected, made Hollywood movers and mainstream fans alike fairly uncomfortable. But Combs's tough image was founded on real-life experience. He was born in Harlem. His mother Janice was a schoolteacher; his father Melvin, a drug dealer, was murdered when Sean was only three years old. Janice told Sean and his sister Keisha that their father had died in a car accident.

When Sean was 12, the family moved to the suburbs, where he entered Mount St. Michael's Academy. A good student, Puffy—who got his nickname as a child because of the way he puffed his cheeks in and out when he lost his temper—played football and spent his free time listening to any and every kind of music. While unsure of what he wanted to be in life, he certainly knew what he didn't want to be. "I never wanted to be average, just one of the billions."[23]

When he was 17, Puffy stumbled upon some old newspaper clippings about his father's shooting. Learning the truth in this way had a profound effect on Sean. It fired his determination to make a success of himself. After high school, he attended Howard University in Washington, D.C., but nothing that the school had to offer interested him. He started dancing in music videos and recalls the day he saw some music executives pull up to a location with their expensive suits, expensive cars, and air of importance. "I remember thinking, I don't know what they do, but I want to do that!"[24]

A short time later Andre Harrell, head of Uptown Records in New York City, recruited Puffy to be an unpaid intern a couple of days a week. Uptown was a four-hour drive from the Howard campus, and the commute was too much. Convinced that the education he wanted couldn't be had at the university and anxious to relocate to New York City, Combs quit school to work full time at Uptown. He rapidly became the company's uber talent scout. It was Combs who discovered Mary J. Blige, Jodeci, Faith Evans, and Notorious B.1.G. Within two years, he'd risen through the ranks to become vice president. Then, in 1993, Puffy was fired from Uptown for "insubordination." But Puffy didn't need Uptown anymore. He signed a deal with Arista Records CEO Clive Davis to start his own label, Bad Boy Records, worth a reported 15 million dollars. Notorious B.1.G. left Uptown and was part of the package. "It was overwhelming, but I had the confidence," Combs later commented, adding that "having one hundred percent faith in God" had always gotten him through. "God, for me, is real. He's somebody I can call on."[25]

And Puffy has found himself in some unholy situations. In 1991, a concert he co-hosted in New York City triggered a stampede that killed nine people, although no charges were brought against him. In 1996, he was convicted of attempted criminal mischief after an altercation with a photographer. He was also charged with assault. Reportedly upset about a music video he'd appeared in, Combs stormed into the Manhattan office of Interscope Records executive Steven Stoute and, along with two bodyguards, allegedly bashed Stoute with a champagne bottle, a chair, and a telephone. The assault charge was dropped after Puffy pleaded guilty to harassment and was ordered to take an anger-management class.

It was widely believed that the rivalry between Combs's Bad Boy label and Suge Knight's Death Row Records—the East Coast-versus-West Coast rap feud—was the impetus behind the still-unsolved murders of Death Row rapper Tupac Shakur and Notorious B.I.G. Shakur died in 1996; and Notorious B.I.G. (real name Christopher Wallace), Combs's best friend and business partner, was gunned down a year later after an L.A. party, which Combs also attended.

Yet Puffy insists that if he has a bad reputation it is the media's fault, calling the rap feud nothing more than media propaganda. He will, however, admit that he is filled with "drive, determination and passion. I've always been confident, borderline cocky. I had a problem with arrogance, but . . . I'm working on correcting it. I have my good, nice, romantic sides and my ugly, angry sides . . . I'm a survivor, a champion, a fighter—but a human being too."[26]

Puffy was also, at that point, a potential career liability for Jennifer, who was busy promoting *Out of Sight*. So, on July 1, a news item was planted indicating that their relationship was cooling. In the Hollywood publicity game it is not uncommon for people on all sides of an issue to "leak" information, or misinformation, to columnists or wire services in order to serve their own interests. According to the Jennifer item, people close to Combs said that although the two remained good friends, the romance part was over. But if Jennifer was at all upset over the alleged breakup, she had shown no signs of it at the *Out of Sight* premiere party the week before.

If the Combs–Lopez romance had really fizzled—and few believed it had—they had done so with admirable congeniality. Not only was Puffy still Jennifer's musical mentor, but he'd also hooked her up with a new manager, Benny Medina.

Her split from longtime manager Eric Gold provoked some rancor. He claimed that once Combs entered Jennifer's life it had become increasingly difficult for him to do his job. "When [Puffy's] around, he's the manager," said Gold. "Whether she takes a movie or not becomes his decision, and when she's with him, she becomes entirely involved. I miss the Jennifer I used to know." But, he added, "She's definitely in love. At the end of the day, she wants to be the mother of his kids."[27]

When *Entertainment Weekly* made Jennifer its cover girl in October 1998, the revealing photograph generated a barrage of mail from the magazine's readers. Some objected to the risqué nature of the photo; others applauded Jennifer for being a trailblazer "in an industry that elevates the likes of Sharon Stone, Julia Roberts, and Gwyneth Paltrow to superstar status within a minute."[28]

While all of these "superstar" leading ladies had endured their share of media interest in their love lives, none of them had to withstand the kind of scrutiny Jennifer was under. Her romance with Combs—were they or weren't they?—became such a hot topic of entertainment-media discussion that Jennifer didn't want to hear about it anymore. "I swear to God . . . I've even trained my family not to call me and tell me what the garbage [in the press] is, because unless they're saying you're killing dogs in the stairway for some religious ritual, it's better not to know." Even Jennifer had to admit, however, that some of the reports were downright comical, such as the one that she'd insured her posterior for one billion dollars. "When I heard the story, I thought it was very funny," Jennifer admitted.[29]

Hoping to exert a little spin control, Jennifer did an interview with *Details*. She flatly denied that she and Puffy were, or had ever been, an item. "Look, Puff and I have hung out and been friends since we did our video, so people started making up all these rumors." When asked directly if she was dating him, Jennifer answered "No."[30]

But her denial wasn't very convincing. Perhaps because everywhere Puffy went, Jennifer was sure to follow. They showed up together in South Beach at a trendy club named Liquid, owned by Madonna's friend Ingrid Casares. When Combs took to the stage for an impromptu performance, Jennifer was right behind him.

At the same time, Jennifer was also putting her celebrity to good use. She participated in a telethon relief effort for the victims of Hurricane Georges, which devastated Puerto Rico, Cuba, and other Caribbean islands in late 1998, killing over 300 people and leaving thousands more homeless. Organized by Gloria and Emilio Estefan, who donated $50,000 of their own money, Jennifer was among the celebrities who participated.

In its December 1998 issue *Details* named Jennifer Lopez the sexiest woman of the year and mentioned her highly publicized behind. Jennifer responded with patience. "I think it started with Selena and all those tight pants. But you know, I don't have to be a size two to be sexy," she told the magazine. "I guess not being ashamed of something like that, which is uncharacteristic of this society, made it become a focal point."[31]

Other celebrities began to make snarky remarks on the record about that famous butt. Supermodel Cindy Crawford remarked to *Self* magazine,

"I don't know if I would have the guts to walk around with that butt . . . Is it cultural, or what was she given in self-confidence that I wasn't?"[32]

There was no denying that 1998 had been a particularly stressful year for Lopez. Insult was added to injury at the second-annual Chuy Awards, which had been created to honor the best—and worst—in Latin entertainment. A year earlier, everyone had been singing Jennifer's praises for her work in *Selena*, but this year she was given a swift kick in her generous butt. The Chuy for the Worst Talk Show Guest Pushing a New Movie went to Jennifer Lopez for her allegedly less-than-scintillating efforts on behalf of *Out of Sight*.

Commenting on the characters she tended to play Jennifer once said, "I don't think of them as strong women. I like characters that are really part of the story as opposed to window dressing; but I think the interesting thing is that they are real people. Nobody walks around being strong all the time."[33] There were times during 1998 that Jennifer could have crumbled, but she didn't. Instead, she learned some hard lessons, the first being to watch was she said and not to elaborate beyond that. She also learned that it would be wise to reach beyond her goal of being a big movie star and explore some new terrain. "I want everything. I want family. I want to do good work. I want love. I want to be comfortable," she confided. "I think of people like Cher and Bette Midler and Diana Ross and Barbra Streisand. That's always been the kind of career I'd hoped to have. I want it all."[34] But she'd get more than she bargained for in the process of attaining it.

NOTES

1. "The 50 Most Beautiful People In The World: Jennifer Lopez." *People*, May 12, 1997, p. 124.

2. Bad Boy Records Press release. November 1997.

3. Stephen Rebello. "The Wow." *Movieline*, February 1998. http://members.aol.com/dafreshprinz/jenniferlopez/movieline0298.htm.

4. Degen Pener. "From Here to Divinity." *Entertainment Weekly*, October 9, 1998.

5. Sony press release, March 1998.

6. Kyle Smith. "To The Top: Shaking It Up." *People*, September 13, 1999, p. 71+.

7. "Page Six," *The New York Post*, May 28, 1998.

8. Cindy Adams. "Cindy's Romantic Dish." *Good Morning America*, June 12, 1998.

9. "Names in the News." *AP Online*, November 14, 1998.

10. Cindy Adams. "Cindy's Romantic Dish." *Good Morning America*, June 12, 1998.

11. Overheard in person by the author.

12. Degen Pener. "Hey, Nude! Hollywood's Fashion Statement." *Style*, June 1998.

13. Stephen Rebello. "The Wow." *Movieline*, February 1998. http://members.aol.com/dafreshprinz/jenniferlopez/movieline0298.htm.

14. Ibid.

15. Ibid.

16. Angelo Figueroa. "Face of Journalism." National Public Radio, June 24, 1998.

17. Degen Pener. "From Here to Divanity." *Entertainment Weekly*, October 9, 1998.

18. Bob Morris. "Line of Fire." *Talk*, March 2000.

19. Degen Pener. "From Here to Divanity." *Entertainment Weekly*, October 9, 1998.

20. Ibid.

21. *Good Morning America*, ABC Television Network, July 6, 1998.

22. Ibid.

23. Stephanie Tuck. "Puff and Stuff: He Came, He Saw, He Redecorated." *In Style*, October 1999.

24. Sophronia Scott Gregory, Sue Miller, and Natasha Stoynoff. "On the Move: The Right Puff." *People*, October 18, 1998.

25. Stephanie Tuck. "Puff and Stuff: He Came, He Saw, He Redecorated." *In Style*, October 1999.

26. Sophronia Scott Gregory, Sue Miller, and Natasha Stoynoff. "On the Move: The Right Puff." *People*, October 18, 1998.

27. Bob Morris. "Line of Fire." *Talk*, March 2000.

28. "Mailbag." *People*, December 21, 1998.

29. Denis Ferrara and Diane Judge. "Puff Daddy's Pal?" *Newsday*, November 22, 1998.

30. Brantley Bardin. "Woman Of The Year: Jennifer Lopez." *Details*, December 1998. http://members.aol.com/dafreshprinz/jenniferlopez/details1298.htm.

31. Ibid.

32. George Rush, Joanna Molloy with Marcus Baram and K. C. Baker. "A Boos Who Of Halloween Ghouls." *NY Post*, November 3, 1998. http://www.nydailynews.com/archives/gossip/1998/11/03/1998-11-03_a_boo_s_who_of_halloween_gho.html. Originally published in *Self* Magazine, October 2000.

33. Degen Pener. "From Here to Divanity." *Entertainment Weekly*, October 9, 1998.

34. Ibid.

Chapter 9

POP STAR

A sure sign that someone has achieved A-list movie star status is when they are invited to lend their voice to a big-budget animated feature. Ever since Disney started delighting—and in some cases terrorizing—children with innovative feature-length cartoons, generations of actors have grown up mesmerized by animation with its boundless imaginative potential. Most jump at the opportunity to be a voice character in a movie; they see it as something they will be able to show to their kids and grandkids with pride.

Antz, released in 1998, was the first animated effort to come out of DreamWorks, a company founded by Stephen Spielberg, music mogul David Geffen, and former Disney executive Jeffrey Katzenberg. Among the voice talent assembled for the film were Woody Allen, Sharon Stone, Sylvester Stallone, Gene Hackman, Dan Aykroyd, Jane Curtin, Danny Glover, and Jennifer Lopez. The story focused on a worker ant named Z (Woody Allen) whose function in life is to be a "soil relocation engineer"—in other words, to dig new tunnels and move dirt. The meaningless nature of his existence makes Z feel insignificant, a concern he shares with his psychiatrist. Jennifer gives vocal life to Z's co-worker Azteca, who tries to make Z understand that his significance lies in his contribution to the colony as a whole.

Voice casting is an interesting exercise. In an animated film, an actor's physical attributes are meaningless and his or her ability to convey personality through voice counts for everything. Antz codirector Eric Darnell said that Jennifer was perfect for Azteca because "she's got this great combination of control and invulnerability—she came from the Bronx and had to hold her own there—and also a certain sort of sensualness that's hard to come by."[1]

Darnell also claimed that getting big names to work on the project wasn't as important to the film's box-office success as people might imagine. "Sure, we get a little press for getting Woody Allen, Gene Hackman and Sharon Stone to do your characters. And it's great to animate these performances, no question about it. But once you get past the recognition, it's the characters that have to keep you interested and involved."[2] And to those who might think supplying the voice for an animated character is an easy way to pick up a fat paycheck, many consider voice-over work the most demanding job an actor can do.

Sandra Bullock, who was the voice of Moses's sister Miriam in the DreamWorks production of *The Prince of Egypt,* says that being alone in a sound booth with no other actors to play off is a little intimidating: "I relate better to people physically, rather than verbally. And for the couple of days I did the recording, I felt so isolated. I've never had this experience before."[3] Anne Bancroft, who was the voice of the queen in *Antz,* called the experience "like being in space. You're acting to this piece of paper in front of you. You have to become a storyteller yourself, because you're required to use your imagination."[4]

But if there was one thing that Jennifer Lopez excelled at it was visualization. As a child she had seen herself as a dancer, and she became one; as a teenager she imagined herself on the big screen, and she pulled it off; now, she was beginning to see herself as a pop star, and she was determined to realize that dream too, despite the strong possibility of failure. Nobody had managed it since Bette Midler—an A-list film actress who could still score a Top 40 hit. But Midler became famous as a singer first, and her hit songs generally came from movie soundtracks. Jennifer intended to establish herself as a singer independent from her work in the movies. When it was pointed out that she was taking a big risk and would perhaps lose some of her hard-earned professional credibility, she was unswayed. "How can I live my life in fear like that? The winners take risks. That's the only way to be. I would hate to be fifty years old and think I should have done that back then."[5]

Jennifer could not have picked a better time for a foray into the music world. If there was a zeitgeist, it had a Latin beat. Suddenly the entire music world was embracing all things Latin. Tommy Mottola was so convinced Latin music was the next big thing that he reportedly earmarked upwards of 10 million dollars to promote Ricky Martin's English-language album and even more to hire top-notch producers like Puff Daddy, entrusting them with the task of guiding Sony's Latin division down the same path country and hip-hop had taken.

St. Clair/Silverthorn 416-393-7709

Toronto Public Library

User ID: 2 ********* 2762

Date Format: DD/MM/YYYY

Number of Items: 1

Item ID:37131033608340
 Title:Jennifer Lopez : a biography
 Date due:17/06/2017

Telephone Renewal# 416-395-5505
www.torontopubliclibrary.ca
 Saturday, May 27, 2017   10:51 AM

. . .

It was a smart investment on Mottola's part. Latin sounds are as old as music itself. Prior to Martin, the most successful crossover Latin artist was Gloria Estefan; she was the first to tap into the potential of Latin music. But the success of Estefan and her husband, Emilio, wasn't fueled entirely by their Latino followers. Through music, they reached across the cultural divide and gathered together non-Hispanics by the arena-full. Like Ricky Martin, the Estefans won people over through hard work and infectious rhythms. They began humbly in the 1970s as the Miami Sound Machine. They scraped by until Sony offered to sign them in 1981. They hit in Latin America first with two Spanish-language albums then they broke through in America with the song "Conga."

Other acts soon followed the energetic lead of the Miami Sound Machine, blending Latin rhythms with dance beats and appealing to Hispanics and Anglos alike. Believing that they'd found the right formula, the Estefans put their life savings towards producing their first English-language album for Sony, *Primitive Love*. Their gamble paid off when it became the first in a string of multiplatinum albums. But the Estefans did more than just ride the wave of their own success. They set out to nurture, develop, and promote other Latin artists. The Estefan's music machine has made them multimillionaires, with their net worth over two hundred million dollars.

So when Jennifer was ready to cross over, recording industry labels were anxious to sign Latino artists, many of whom became ubiquitous by the late 1990s. In the middle of Hollywood, a huge headshot of Enrique Iglesias peered from a billboard promoting the local Spanish-language radio station. Luis Miguel, another Latin pop singer, sold more than 12 million copies of the first two albums in his Warner Music *Romance* trilogy. Another gauge of Latin music's popularity is its dance-club domination, not only in America but also around the world.

When Jennifer first decided to pursue a music career, she originally planned to do it in Spanish. "I did a demo in Spanish after *Selena* and submitted it to the Work label," she recalls. "They said, 'We like it, but we want you to do it in English.'"[6]

So although Jennifer wasn't a Spanish-language performer trying to cross over, and even though her sounds were decidedly mainstream pop, she clearly benefited from the surge of interest in Latino artists. It didn't hurt, either, that she was constantly being singled out for one honor or another. Once again, in 1999, *People* magazine inscribed her on their 50 Most Beautiful People list. This time, Jennifer told her *People* interviewer that to her beauty is an aspect of self-assurance and credited her parents for instilling that in her. "Every time I call, my dad says, 'Hi, gorgeous.' That makes me feel beautiful." Jennifer was also happy to be a poster girl for the voluptuous. "For so long it was just skinny, skinny, skinny. I'm glad to contribute to the self-esteem of others."[7]

Originally, Jennifer was going to call her album *Gypsy*, a reference to her days as a dancer. In the end, though, she chose to pay homage to the train that carried her into New York to chase her dreams so she titled the album *On the 6*. Sony backed up the project with some serious and expensive talent: Puffy Combs and Emilio Estefan, who had guided his wife Gloria to the top of the charts so many times, were two of Jennifer's producers.

As the album's release date neared, Sony got the publicity machine going full throttle. They arranged for Jennifer Lopez and Ricky Martin to do a photo shoot together, hoping that some of the frenzy surrounding Martin's debut English-language album would rub off on Jennifer. Puffy accompanied Jennifer to the Manhattan studio where the shoot took place, and he watched as she posed seductively with the handsome young performer whose album had debuted at number one on the *Billboard* chart. Jennifer's own album was due to be released the following week. She told *Newsweek* that "it's always a good time to be Latin," but now, she added, "the world is starting to see what it's like to grow up in a Latin family: the flavor and the culture and the passion and the music. We're a very passionate people."[8]

Despite remarks such as these, however, *On the 6* was less about passion and more about safe commercialism. Production values were slick, and the cuts contained carefully measured amounts of R & B and Latin rhythms. Unlike Martin's last Spanish-language album, *Vuelve*, which had won him a Grammy, *On the 6* was no ground breaker.

In a *Vibe* interview Jennifer declared, "I can't try to be Whitney or Faith. I do something different. I have something else to offer to anybody who'll want to, you know, f***ing get down."[9] In the same interview, Big Pun, who worked with Jennifer on an Puffy-produced album track called "Feeling So Good," said that Jennifer "represents all the things that [Latinos] are: beautiful, voluptuous, intelligent, proud."[10]

One interesting side note about Jennifer Lopez and Ricky Martin is that at the time of their photo shoot, Jennifer was in negotiations to make a new film version of the classic Broadway musical *West Side Story*. "Natalie Wood needed makeup to play a Puerto Rican girl in the original [film version]," Jennifer noted. "I have been fighting to play characters written white, but this is one time I will proudly play ethnic. I long for the day when Hollywood will truly be color blind."[11] Martin was also approached about the project, but, unlike Jennifer, who had a sentimental place in her heart for the musical, Martin showed no interest in updating the classic, telling *Newsweek,* "It would represent gangs and stereotypes about my culture."[12]

So, if the *West Side Story* project was to proceed, it would have to do so without the then-king of Latin heartthrobs. And of more immediate concern to Jennifer than these project negotiations was her album. At least on the surface, she could not have asked for a more auspicious debut. *On the 6* made history by hitting number one on the Hot 100, Hot 100 Singles Sales, and R & B Singles Sales charts simultaneously. "If You Had My Love," the album's first single, headed to the top of the pop charts. Jennifer, who co-wrote three of the songs on the album, chatted about her craft with *In Style:* "You have to have heightened emotions. If you're really happy, angry, depressed or in love, you can write a good song."[13]

And, apparently, Jennifer was feeling ecstatic. Her album, which would eventually go on to achieve double-platinum status, was being promoted with all the ferocity Sony could muster, and she was the latest darling of the musical world. In May, she and singer Marc Anthony—with whom she'd sung a ballad on the album—appeared together at the record release party for *On the 6* at the Manhattan nightclub Float. The *New York Daily News* implied that Anthony and Jennifer were now a romantic item, although the reporter acknowledged that Jennifer had, in fact, spent most of the evening dancing with a variety of partners, including model Taye Diggs and baseball star Derek Jeter.

The hype onslaught that Sony had orchestrated for *On the 6* seemed to counterbalance the generally poor reviews the record received. In a lengthy critique, *Entertainment Weekly* gave it a C grade. "Despite an all-star cast, Jennifer Lopez's singing isn't out-of-sight," wrote David Browne. He also pointed out that despite all those high-profile producers who had been brought into the project—"all recruited to add heft to Lopez's career makeover"—the problem was that "as soon as Lopez opens her mouth . . . all this advance work falls by the wayside."[14]

Browne also described her voice as being higher and thinner than expected—"not embarrassing, but sadly ordinary." He also considered the album's ballads "prissy" and the dance cuts "tame." As far as he was concerned, only "Waiting for Tonight" stood out—a cut "worthy of a dance floor diva." Browne concluded by predicting that 20 years down the road "this album will be part of someone's doctoral thesis on the dangers of crossover. For all the wads of money spent on her fledging musical career, Lopez comes across as little more than a Mild Spice Girl."[15]

Wall of Sound reviewer Daniel Durchholz echoed Browne. "Producers and guest stars can only do so much, and there are problems with the material and with Lopez's own performances that make *On the 6* an ultimately disappointing effort. In the first place, though it's never wincingly bad, her voice is weak." Durchholz also took issue with the production of the songs, pointing to the spoken-word section of "Should've Never," where he said Lopez "whispers and coos in Spanish like a Puerto Rican reincarnation of Claudine Longet. It's supposed to be sexy, of course, but Latin pop is full of such overwrought moments."[16]

Ben Werner of the *Orange County Register* had some kinder words for Jennifer herself, noting she could sing but he went on to skewer the song lyrics, calling them horrendous.

In his overview of the new crop of Latin performers, Mike Usinger of the Web site InfoCulture was hard on Jennifer. "As laughable as the ballads are, the rest of *On the 6* isn't much better . . . Simply because she's Latin, Lopez is going to end up one of the most overplayed artists of the summer. Yes, she may look great, but I want a little substance with my sex appeal. And if I'm going to buy into the Latin craze I want a full blown fiesta. Quite frankly, I don't think Lopez would know a pina colada from a pinata."[17]

Entertainment Weekly's Betty Cortina picked up the she-may-be-Latin-but-her-music-isn't theme, applying it to Martin, as well. "While Martin and Lopez are bona fide Latinos (he from the balmy beaches of Puerto Rico, she from the balmy borough of the Bronx, N.Y.), their current hit albums are unapologetic pop. Save for a brassy horn riff here and a Spanish-guitar fill there, the music's as Latin as, say, George Michael or Janet Jackson."[18] In fact, a number of other artists were also being accused of jumping on the Latin bandwagon, including Puffy, who included a Spanish song on one of his own albums. Combs's representatives insisted the track was Puffy's gesture of appreciation for his Latino fans.

Through all of this, as the critics complained and *On the 6* flew off record-store shelves, Jennifer and Puffy hung together. Finally, in the summer of 1999, *Star* magazine reported that Jennifer and Combs had finally gone public with their romance at her 29th birthday party held on July 24 at New York City's Halo Club. Guests at the star-studded celebration—including Leonardo DiCaprio, Derek Jeter, Donald Trump, Vivica A. Fox, Stephen Baldwin, and Queen Latifah—ate bright-pink birthday cake and watched Jennifer and Puffy kiss and cuddle in a corner.

But while their private lives may have been blissful, Combs's accelerating career was hitting some unexpected bumps. A number of artists on his label were upset that Combs only seemed interested in promoting his own albums, leaving them to simmer on the back burner. "I applaud Puffy's success," Faith Evans told Johnnie Roberts of *Newsweek*. "But I do feel it took away a lot of attention in terms of work and thought put into other artists. His time availability isn't the same. A lot of artists aren't happy."[19] In fact, one prominent group, the top-selling rap outfit called The Lox, defected and signed with Interscope, citing a combination of irreconcilable differences. Some members of the Puff Daddy camp claimed that Combs was distracted by Jennifer.

Combs, however, maintained that he was on top of the situation, and the fun and games continued. On August 25, the *New York Post's* "Page Six" gossip section revealed that Combs had "interviewed" Jennifer Lopez for his magazine, *Notorious* and published a brief excerpt. Among other things, Combs asked Jennifer about the type of guy she likes ("a tough exterior, but sweet inside"). Any lingering doubts that Jennifer and Sean were officially together were dispelled by September. The *New York Daily News* reported on September 7 that at Puffy's annual White Party, held at his Easthampton estate, he and Jennifer had held hands and danced together. "For a couple who are notoriously elusive about the state of their relationship, they left no doubt that they are very together," remarked one witness.[20] The game of cat and mouse appeared to be over at last.

The question of what Jennifer's next career move would be was also answered when it was announced that she had signed a five-million-dollar deal to costar with Vince Vaughn, of *The Lost World* and *Swingers*, in a thriller called *The Cell*. It looked as though her recording career would flourish, as well: she received four MTV Video Music Award nominations for the "If You Had My Love" video.

Jennifer would be prominently featured at the televised awards ceremonies, but some of the recognition she received had little to do with respect for her music. During his opening monologue, host Chris Rock made Jennifer the butt, so to speak, of some harsh jokes. "Jennifer Lopez here tonight, Jennifer Lopez. She came with two limos, one for her and one for her ass. I love Jennifer. Where you at girl? You don't thank your ass enough. I see Jennifer on TV thanking her momma and daddy and her acting coach. Thank your ass girl, thank your ass, before your ass goes solo, 'cause the ass is the star of the show. Jennifer is just the Commodores—her ass is Lionel Ritchie."[21] Later that night Jennifer infuriated reporter Jorge Estevez of New York's News 12 the Bronx by backing out of a promised interview. Estevez retaliated by leading off his story with the item that Jennifer had been shut out at the awards, losing in all four categories in which she had been nominated.

On December 5, at the fifth annual VH1/Vogue Fashion Awards in New York City, hosted by Heather Locklear and Puff Daddy, Jennifer fared better, being voted Most Fashionable Female Artist. Her dress—a gold, cleavage displaying Gucci gown by designer of the year Tom Ford—was also a hit. But Jennifer made it clear that to her wearing revealing clothes was a fashion, not a moral, statement. "People equate sexy with promiscuous," she said. "They think that because I'm shaped this way, I must be scandalous like running around and bringing men into my hotel room. But it's just the opposite."[22]

Jennifer had always maintained that she was a one-man woman, and now, it appeared, Combs was ready to be a one-woman man. Rush and Molloy reported that at his November 1999 birthday bash Combs had told his friends, "I never had anyone love me the way she loves me. I love her and, hopefully, one day I will be able to marry her."[23] Jennifer wasn't there to hear these sweet words because she was in Los Angeles filming *The Cell*. She did, however, send Puffy videotaped birthday wishes in which she dressed up as Marilyn Monroe, complete with blond wig and tight dress, and sang "Happy Birthday," just like Marilyn did for President Kennedy. Rumors then began circulating that Puffy and Jennifer were planning a New Year's Eve wedding in Miami.

In December 1999, *People* magazine included Jennifer on its 25 Most Intriguing People of 1999 list. The accompanying article reported that Jennifer's representatives denied the engagement. It also offered this insight from *Cell* producer Julio Caro who observed Jennifer was "just not someone who will do the obvious or logical choice. She's always pushing that envelope."[24]

NOTES

1. Degen Pener. "From Here to Divinity." *Entertainment Weekly*, October 9, 1998.

2. Gene Seymour. "Acting Animated." *Newsday*, December 13, 1998.

3. Ibid.

4. Ibid.

5. Degen Pener. "From Here to Divinity." *Entertainment Weekly*, October 9, 1998.

6. Veronica Chambers and John Leland. "Lovin' La Vida Loca." *Newsweek*, May 31, 1999.

7. "The 25 Most Intriguing People of '99." *People*, December 31, 1999.

8. Veronica Chambers and John Leland. "Lovin' La Vida Loca." *Newsweek*, May 31, 1999, p. 72.

9. "Dream Hampton." *Vibe*, August, 1999.

10. Ibid.

11. Louis B. Hobson. "Latino Actors Still Fighting for Respect." *London Free Press*, July 8, 1999.

12. Veronica Chambers and John Leland. "Lovin' La Vida Loca." *Newsweek*, May 31, 1999, p. 72.

13. Editorial Staff. *In Style*, June 1999.

14. David Browne. *Entertainment Weekly*, June 4, 1999.

15. Ibid.

16. Daniel Durchholz. *Wall of Sound*, June 1999.

17. Mike Usinger. InfoCulture.com. http://infoculture.cbc.ca/archives/musop/musop_06241999_martinreview.html.

18. Betty Cortina. "The Other Chili Peppers." *Entertainment Weekly*, July 9, 1999.

19. Johnnie L. Roberts. "Puffy's Crowded Orbit." *Newsweek*, November 8, 1999.

20. George Rush and Joanna Malloy. "Rush and Molloy," *New York Daily News*, May 27, 1999.

21. Author was present at Awards and heard monologue, September 9, 1999 at Metropolitan Opera House, New York City.

22. VH1 Fashion Awards, New York City, December 5, 1999.

23. "The 25 Most Intriguing People of '99." *People*, December 31, 1999.

24. Rush and Molloy. *New York Daily News*, December 24, 1999.

Chapter 10

TARNISHED IMAGE

It sometimes seemed that Jennifer was genetically incapable of keeping a low profile. In November 1999, *People* ran an item about trouble on the set of her new film, *The Cell*, in which she plays a child psychologist who enters the mind of a comatose serial killer. The film includes several fantasy or dream sequences for which Lopez had to wear a number of wigs. *People*'s Tom Cunneff reported that the film's original hairdresser left the project soon after filming began. She claimed that she hadn't been allowed to speak directly to Jennifer and was required to communicate through intermediaries. Producer Julio Caro denied this, explaining that the hairdresser had left because her experience with wigs was insufficient. "There's a big difference between hair and wigs," Caro told Cunneff, adding, "Jennifer is quite accessible. She has an assistant on the set, but we all communicate directly with her."[1]

Finding people she could trust became more challenging for Lopez. Other than her assistant, Arlene, with whom she had been friends since grade school, there were few people she could count on to be discrete. Even her ex-husband Ojani Noa had let her down. He did a tell-all interview with the British tabloid *News of the World* for a hefty sum in which he described his dramatic escape from Cuba on a balsa-wood raft and claimed that Jennifer had picked him up while he was a waiter. The American tabloid *Globe* picked up where the *News* left off, running its own story under the screaming headline *Sex-Crazed Jennifer Lopez Dumped Me*. It was Jennifer, he insisted in the article, who proposed to him—and who wanted out of the marriage a few months later.[2]

Shortly before Christmas 1999, the New York gossip columnists couldn't make up their minds about Combs and Lopez. Were they planning on living happily ever after or on the verge of splitting up? Depending upon which newspaper you read and on what day, either Puffy was going to dump Jennifer because she was too assertive for his taste or he was presenting her with a mink coat and an antique diamond bracelet. Then there were the anonymous sources who claimed it was Jennifer who was trying to break away from Combs.

One thing was certain, however: on December 26, 1999, the two were very much together at Club New York on West 43rd Street in Manhattan. By the next morning three people would be hospitalized and Jennifer would find herself immersed in the biggest scandal of her life. There are as many versions of what happened at Club New York that night as there are witnesses. But a scan of police and news reports yields this account:

Puffy and Jennifer were at the club accompanied by one of Puffy's Bad Boy artists, Shyne, a 19-year-old rapper whose real name is Jamal Barrow; Puffy's bodyguard, Anthony "Wolf" Jones, considered by many of Puffy's friends to be the type of companion Combs should have been removing from his life; and a group of about 30 friends. According to several eyewitnesses, Combs was flaunting his wealth by tossing wads of cash around to the annoyance of some of the club's other patrons—it was later determined that he was carrying about eight thousand dollars. They eventually confronted him, and one man threw a stack of bills back at Combs.

It was then that Combs allegedly brandished a gun. Normally anyone entering the club has to pass through metal detectors, but because Puffy was a VIP neither he nor anyone with him was required to suffer the indignity of waiting in line or being scanned for weaponry. After Combs allegedly pulled out a gun, so did Shyne. The young rapper then opened fire with his 9 mm Ruger. "Everybody hit the floor and people started screaming," reported a witness. "It was pandemonium."[3] Three bystanders were hit; a woman was shot in the face and two men were struck in the shoulder. Miraculously, no one was fatally wounded.

In the confusion and panic that immediately ensued, Combs and Lopez fled from the scene in his Lincoln Navigator SUV, along with his driver and bodyguard Jones, an ex-convict who had once been imprisoned for shooting at a cop. According to the Manhattan prosecutor assigned to the case, Puffy and Jennifer attempted to evade the pursuing police, running at least 10 red lights in the process. When officers finally succeeded in pulling their car over, they claimed to have discovered a stolen 9 mm in the vehicle.[4] Everyone was taken into custody.

Lopez was held for almost 14 hours, reportedly handcuffed to a bench, and she spent the early-morning hours of December 27 weeping uncontrollably. But one of Puffy's lawyers, Ed Hayes, later denied that Jennifer had broken down. "She's a capable person and despite what was in the tabloids she was not hysterical that night," Hayes said. "When I was talking to her she had tremendous focus and charisma and if she appeared to be a mess, it was only as a way to manipulate the cops. Of course she cried, but that didn't mean she didn't have total control of the situation."[5]

Hayes did admit, however, that Lopez was very concerned about how her mother would react to the situation, and at one point she commented, "My mother's going to be so upset."[6]

In the end, she was cleared of any wrongdoing. Outside the precinct house, Jennifer's lawyer, Larry Ruggiero, made this statement to a crowd of reporters: "Jennifer Lopez, who was detained and questioned by police today at the 35th precinct in NYC, has been exonerated of all charges connected to the possession of an illegal firearm. Jennifer has been released . . . Ms. Lopez was detained and questioned and fully cooperated with authorities. Jennifer Lopez does not own a firearm nor does she condone the use of firearms."[7]

In court that morning for Combs's arraignment, the prosecutor admitted that the witnesses he'd lined up were willing to testify that they'd only seen Combs pull out a gun; nobody would say they actually saw him shoot it. Combs's attorney Harvey Siovis argued before the judge that it was not only false but also illogical to assert that his client was guilty of either brandishing a weapon or firing it. "Jennifer Lopez is a very famous actress," Siovis said. "And to think Mr. Combs is walking with Miss Lopez with a loaded gun, and he is not the shooter, and then left. He goes to the car, and he still has the gun. It's ridiculous." The attorney also pointed out that the gun had been found in the front of the Navigator and that "it's not reasonable to charge the people in the back."[8] Bail was finally set at $10,000, and Combs was freed.

The pistol found in the Navigator had been reported stolen in August from a pickup truck in suburban Atlanta. Officials at the Bureau of Alcohol, Tobacco and Firearms and the New York police said that the 9 mm Smith & Wesson model 915 was the same one reported stolen by a construction worker named Ralph Cooper, of Powder Springs, Cobb County, Georgia. "He hadn't seen the gun for about a month and then reported it missing. A cell phone was also taken from the truck," Powder Springs police Sergeant Matt Atkins explained.[9]

If there was ever a time for Lopez to cut her losses and run as fast as she could away from Combs, it was now. Instead, she seemed more determined than ever to stand beside him. After their release she and Combs went back to their room at the Peninsula Hotel. There they prepared for the inevitable fallout. The next day, they met with Siovis and Puffy's publicist, Dan Klores, to work out what Combs would say at a scheduled press conference. According to *Talk*'s Michael Daly, it was Lopez who insisted he maintain that he had no gun. When the time came to face the press, Combs looked positively collegiate in an understated pullover sweater and slacks. He made his statement. "On Sunday evening, I went to Club New York. Under no circumstances whatsoever did I have anything to do with a shooting. I do not own a gun, nor did I possess a gun, that night. I want to make this one-hundred-percent clear. I had nothing to do with a shooting in this club, and I feel terrible that people were hurt that night. I'm positive, in the next couple of days, due to the investigation, that the truth will come out."[10]

In January 2000, Combs was indicted and charged with two counts of criminal possession of a weapon. A month later prosecutors added one count of bribing a witness—the driver of the Navigator, Wardel Fenderson deepened his former employer's legal woes by telling police that Puffy tried to bribe him to say that the gun found in the Navigator was his. According to Fenderson, Combs offered him $50,000 in cash and a diamond ring—which was a birthday present given to Combs by Lopez.[11] "I am outraged by this new charge," Combs said in a statement. "I am not guilty. From the outset I have firmly believed that the Manhattan district attorney's office has unfairly targeted me for baseless charges."[12] The bribery charge carries a penalty of seven years in prison.

Dan Klores, however, vehemently denied the gun belonged to Combs and called his client a victim of circumstance who was fleeing a life-threatening situation. Combs's bodyguard Jones and Fenderson also faced weapons charges.

Shyne was indicted on the most serious charges: attempted murder, assault, criminal use of a firearm, reckless endangerment, and criminal possession of a weapon. It was not his first run-in with the law. The would-be rapper sensation was trouble just waiting to happen. Shortly after signing with Bad Boy, Shyne crashed his new Mercedes, and the accident resulted in the death of a friend. Then, just a few months before the club shooting, Shyne was involved in a fight; afterwards, an unidentified individual shot at him in Puffy's recording studio. "Puffy has to address issues of personal growth and change," Klores told *Newsweek*. "Then you can begin to address the matter of people's perception of him."[13]

The shooting brought Puffy under intense media scrutiny. Articles came out rehashing his (allegedly) past violent encounters and less savory activities. As Puffy's life was being dissected, so was Jennifer's. But in her case the media generally stuck to the theme of "What's a nice girl like this doing with a bad guy like that?" Even before the shooting, Lopez was under a lot of pressure from her circle to separate herself from Combs. A close friend of Jennifer's told *Newsweek* "The people around her were worried that something like this would happen. They have repeatedly told her that you can't be Hollywood's sweetheart if you're running from the cops."[14] Another told *Entertainment Weekly*, "She's old enough to know better. Everyone should make a New Year's wish for her that she finds a new boyfriend."[15]

Of course, there was the not-so-small matter of Jennifer's heart. As another friend of Jennifer's put it, "It's tough for her because she does really love Puffy. He has what she likes—determination and aggressiveness. But she also knows it might be a choice between a doomed relationship and a doomed career."[16]

Jennifer herself says she likes excitement and has a definite wild side, "I fire up very easily. I don't drink or do drugs or even smoke, but I'm still the one who will get up on a table and dance."[17] She also longs to remarry, settle down, and have children. She has a very strong sense of family, which is why buying a Los Angeles home was so symbolic for her. "There's only one place you go—home." Lopez says she always takes comfort in the understanding that "no matter what else happens, knowing that my whole family could live in the house the rest of our lives is the best feeling in the world."[18]

She dismissed suggestions that she was just a Puffy puppet and says she is where *she* wants to be. "Nobody really forces me to do anything. That could be one of the best things about me and it could be one of the worst, I don't know."[19] Living such a busy, and such a public life, taught Jennifer the importance of being alone. "You get to listen to you, to the voices in your head. I think that's what we avoid a lot of times because it's usually the truth and the truth is hard to deal with."[20]

Jennifer's way of dealing with the shooting and the fallout from it was to keep moving forward and to immerse herself in work. After wrapping *The Cell*, she started filming a romantic comedy called *The Wedding Planner*, opposite Matthew McConaughey. She described the experience as the most fun she's ever had on a movie set. Lopez also busied herself by making more fashion headlines at the 2000 Grammys. Her Versace palm-print silk chiffon dress somehow managed to make her look more naked than she'd be if she had worn nothing at all. Lopez maintains that she had no idea—really—that the gown would cause such a media stir. "I thought it was a beautiful dress," she protested, then laughed. "When

I came out [to present an award] they were all shocked and appalled."[21] Her co-presenter, X-Files star David Duchovny, quipped, "Jennifer, this is the first time in five or six years I'm sure nobody is looking at me." After Lopez left the stage, Rosie O'Donnell, who hosted the ceremonies, meowed, "It's nice to see Jennifer in a classy little understated number like that. And she wonders why people make fun of her body."[22] Actually, few members of the audience appeared to be making fun. But there were plenty of dropped jaws.

For days afterwards, newspapers and television entertainment shows ran photos of Lopez in that sheer, cut-to-the-navel dress. Everyone was asking, "How did she keep it from falling open and revealing all?" Lopez supplied the answer in a TV interview—toupee tape. "It wasn't going to move," she said. "It didn't seem that out there to me. It was a good-looking dress. It wasn't as open as it looked on TV. I had no idea it was going to be such a big deal."[23]

In late March, Jennifer appeared on Access Hollywood and talked about her relationship with Combs without ever once saying his name. She admitted that they had been going through some rough times, but she seemed determined to move forward. "We're not through it yet. Hopefully, everything will come out okay. We have each other. There are ups and downs. You make the best of it." As for the future, "I do want to have kids and I do want to get married," she said. "Who knows if it will be anytime soon."[24]

Jennifer continued to stand by Puffy and in the end, experienced little if any professional fallout. Her L'Oreal spokesperson deal remained intact, the movie roles kept coming, and she proceeded with plans for a new album. As far as her personal life, she was determined to follow her heart. "I really trust myself; I trust my instincts," she says. "My heart is the ruler of all my being—who I am, where I want to be, who I want to be with. If my heart tells me it's true and right, then that's good enough for me."[25]

In February 2001, her heart told her the relationship with Combs had run its course. On Valentine's Day, Puffy issued a statement through his publicist that he and Lopez had officially split. "Mr. Combs confirmed that he and his love Jennifer Lopez have in fact broken up. Mr. Combs is confirming this today as he wanted to put all the rumors surrounding their relationship to rest. At this difficult time we ask that you respect his privacy."[26]

A month later, Combs would be acquitted of all charges related to the club shooting. Shyne was found guilty of reckless endangerment and assault and was sentenced to 10 years in prison. And Jennifer walked away feeling wiser for her time with Puffy. In a May 2001 Latina interview Jennifer said that women "give up so much in a relationship . . . we tend to give away all our power, because we love so completely." The feature she was shooting, Enough, struck a particular chord with Lopez. Her character is an abused woman and the movie's main message is about "finding balance—loving someone, but still being an individual . . . even on smaller levels, like being in a relationship that you know you shouldn't be in. It's about not losing yourself in a relationship; about going, 'I deserve this. I'm a person, too.'"[27]

But it would still be awhile before Jennifer found the relationship that would give her the balance she yearned for.

NOTES

1. Tom Cunneff. "Insider." *People*, November 1, 1999. http://www.people.com/people/archive/article/0,,20129614,00.html.

2. Patrice Baldwin. "Sex-Crazed Jennifer Lopez Dumped Me! After Only 15 Months, Says Ex-Hubby." *Globe*, January 4, 2000.

3. Tom Sinclair. "Daddy Oh!" *Entertainment Weekly*, January 7, 2000.

4. Ibid.

5. Bob Morris. "Could This be Love?" *Talk Magazine*, March 2000. http://beautiful962.yuku.com/topic/4034/t/Talk-Magazine-March-2000.html.

6. Ibid.

7. Press release from Alan Nierob, December 27, 1999.

8. Johnnie L. Roberts and Allison Samuels. "Under the Gun." *Newsweek*, January 10, 2000. http://www.newsweek.com/id/98453.

9. "Gun found in rapper's car was stolen in Cobb County." *Tampa Bay Online*, December 29, 1999. http://tampabayonline.net/news/news102j.htm.

10. Michael Daly. *Talk*, March 2000. http://archives.cnn.com/1999/SHOWBIZ/Music/12/28/combs.conf.

11. AP wire report, February 24, 2000.

12. Ibid.

13. Johnnie L. Roberts and Allison Samuels. *Newsweek*, January 10, 2000.

14. Ibid.

15. Tom Sinclair. "Daddy Oh!" *Entertainment Weekly*, January 7, 2000.

16. PRNewswire, January 2, 2000.

17. Martha Frankel. "Jennifer Lopez Loves To . . ." *Cosmopolitan*, March 1999.

18. MTV Diary, March 29, 2000.

19. Ibid.

20. Ibid.

21. *Entertainment Tonight*, March 6, 2000.

22. Grammy broadcast, February 23, 2000.

23. *Entertainment Tonight*, March 6, 2000.

24. *Access Hollywood*, March 21, 2000.

25. MTV Diary, March 29, 2000.

26. "It's Splitsville for Puffy and J.Lo," CNN. February 14, 2001.

27. "You go, J.Lo," *Latina*, June 2001, pp. 80–86.

Chapter 11

A NEW CHAPTER

In April 2001, Lopez traveled to the United Kingdom to promote *The Wedding Planner*. Co-starring Matthew McConaughey, the film was a romantic comedy about a career-driven wedding planner who finds love with the most unlikely man—the groom-to-be of the wedding she's planning. During an interview with an Irish newspaper, Jennifer denied she was the difficult femme fatale she felt the media portrayed her with reports like her refusing to get in a silver limo for the MTV awards because she ordered a grey one or that her fee for performing at functions was a steep $750,000. Adding to her reputation as a prima donna was Jennifer's alleged demands while appearing on the British variety show *Top of the Pops*, which included requesting "ten dressing rooms, decorated in ruffled lace, white silk, white furniture and white orchids and having three personal chefs flown in to make sure she was eating properly."[1]

Jennifer claimed she was genuinely a down-to-earth person and not spoiled. "I'm very goofy in real life," she insisted. "I love to make jokes and make people laugh. That's just who I am. I see myself as a glamorous movie star, and I see myself as a little hip hop girl from the Bronx and I see myself as a rock 'n' roll person. I have different sides."[2]

Jennifer said she avoided reading the papers too much so was only vaguely aware of her public image. "When Selena came out it was a struggle to adjust to being watched by the world . . . You really just have to pull back and go, 'Aren't I still the same person that I was when I was living in the Bronx and sleeping with my sisters, the three of us in one bed?' Yes, I am."[3]

She claimed to have much more in common with her film character than with the diva image she had been saddled with. "When I signed on to do *The Wedding Planner* my life mirrored my character because I was so focused on my career. I put my love life on the back burner."[4]

And in early 2001 her career was hotter than ever. In addition to her album, she now commanded $9 million per movie, had just announced a new clothing line in association with Tommy Hilfiger's younger brother Andy and was developing a TV series for NBC about her life growing up in the Bronx's tough Castle Hill neighborhood. But her personal life was heating up, too. Whatever the factors that led to her break-up with Combs, Lopez was not gun-shy about jumping into another serious relationship. By March 2001, just a month after her break-up with Combs, she showed up at the Academy Awards with dancer/choreographer Cris Judd, whom she recently met when he was hired to work on her "Love Don't Cost a Thing" music video. In June, Cris proposed while they were at a barbecue and Jennifer accepted.

Lopez shrugged off concerns from friends that she was rushing down the aisle. She told a reporter her failed first marriage taught her that a marriage required more than just love to succeed—it also needed compromise and sacrifice.

"Although I am very into my work and love what I do and I'm always going to strive to be the best I can be, know that at the end of the day, it's not going to bring me the happiness I need or the tranquility or the peace of mind."[5]

Nor did her divorce from Noa make her cynical. "Nothing has changed me or made me bitter or jaded. You have a fairytale idea of life when you are a little girl—and I still believe it."[6]

Fairytales notwithstanding, Jennifer is a clear-eyed realist when it comes to business. "If men are ambitious, it's the most wonderful thing in the world. But in this society if you say 'ambitious' about a woman, it's like a dirty word. But I don't let anybody tell me what I can and can't do. If I want something and I want to go after it, I don't let anything hold me back from it."[7]

That said, Jennifer believes her media image has unfairly affected directors' and studios' perceptions of her. "In the beginning, I was a blank slate. I got to work with all these great directors because I was just a girl who came in there and did well in the audition. Then when I became famous, I was being offered movies that I could star in but that's all I was being offered. When I think I should be seeing the big directors, they don't even consider me. They see me as a sexy singer and too much in the media. It's something I have to combat. Unless they sit in a room with you, and they see you can be a blank slate or be that character when you walk into a room, then they won't even think of you,"[8] she complains. "Now it's harder for me to get in with the really big directors."[9]

But when it comes to relationships, Jennifer claims she's a traditional, old-fashioned lady. "I've never asked a guy out on a date," she says. "I think the perfect man is somebody . . . understanding about what I do for a living. Somebody who's gentle and kind but still has strength . . . I'm very open with my love. I'm passionate . . . I'm not afraid of love. Romance is not so much the expensive things—it's the little things. It's the notes. It's the call in the middle of the day when you're stressed out."[10]

Lopez and Judd were married in September 2001. The ceremony was a non-denominational service and was a glamorous affair attended only by family and close friends. Jennifer's two sisters were bridesmaids, and her best friend from the Bronx, Arlene Rodriguez, served as maid of honor. The couple's first dance was to Stevie Wonder's "Ribbon in the Sky" and the reception lasted until after 2 A.M. with guests dancing to salsa and meringue music.

A month later her debut clothing collection debuted. Made mostly of denim, the moderately priced pieces ranged from sexy casual to sporty chic and were intended for young women between 16 and 25. In the planning stages was a clothing line for pre-teens scheduled for the spring of 2002 and an adult swimwear line.

While her professional life was running smoothly, cracks already began showing in her new marriage by April 2002. According to a report in *The Mirror* newspaper, Jennifer had asked Cris to stay off the set of her new film *Gigli* when she was scheduled to shoot love scenes with co-star Ben Affleck, who was uncomfortable at the thought of Judd being there to watch.[11]

In late May *Us* magazine ran a cover story on Jennifer. In it she said, "Chris brings serenity into my world. In the midst of the crazy storm that is my life, his love is what I need most of all."[12]

A week later, on June 7, 2002, the Associated Press reported that Lopez and Judd had separated. Soon after it was revealed that Lopez was involved with Ben Affleck; by November they were engaged after Affleck presented Jennifer with a $1.2 million pink diamond. The couple was dubbed "Bennifer" and they topped the Most Wanted list of seemingly every paparazzo the world over. The media and public interest was white hot. When Lopez was on location in New York during December 2002 filming *Maid in Manhattan*, throngs of crowding fans and hordes of photographers delayed filming.

Although Jennifer usually maintained that she tried to ignore outside influence, she admitted the media glare was blinding. "I think it's kind of at a fever pitch right now. It's kind of strange. I've gone through my period where it was so surreal and weird," she said. "And it made me feel like kind of a panda in the zoo. It makes you freak out a bit. I've learned to realize that along with my job, which I happen to love very much, this is part of it. You kind of have to adjust and deal with it or you won't be happy."[13]

Both Ben and Jennifer said publicly they wanted to have children. "Jen and I want to get married for the same reason everyone else does: We fell in love," Affleck said in February 2003. "I want to have a family; and she's the only person I've ever met who made me entertain the thought of that. You know within 10 minutes of meeting her she'd be a good mother. Jen has had fewer boyfriends than your average high school junior. She's extremely chaste. There's a kind of language that's used about her—the spicy Latina, the tempestuous diva. She's characterized as oversexed. The woman's had five boyfriends in her whole life! She's a deeply misunderstood woman in my opinion."[14]

Lopez and Affleck announced a September 13, 2003 wedding, taking place in Santa Barbara. But days before the planned ceremony, the couple abruptly postponed the wedding, claiming the media intrusion had forced them to reschedule. Instead, they officially broke off the engagement in January 2004.

Jennifer also hit professional bumps. The constant media attention on "Bennifer" turned Lopez into the butt of pop culture jokes by late night talk show hosts. Where she had once been seen first and foremost as one of Hollywood's brightest talents, her private life overshadowed her acting. Even more damaging, both *Gigli* and her next film, *Jersey Girl*, were critical and box office flops. Add to that her reputation as a diva and Jennifer was no longer Hollywood's golden girl.

That June Lopez surprised many by marrying singer Marc Anthony—four days after his divorce from Puerto Rican actress and former Miss Universe Dayanara Torres Delgado was final. Anthony and Delgado have two children; Marc has another daughter from a previous relationship.

Jennifer and Marc were married in a secret ceremony on June 5, 2004 at her home in Beverly Hills, California. The guests who attended thought they were going to a house party. The newlyweds enjoyed a brief honeymoon at the San Ysidro Ranch near Santa Barbara, California. Almost a year to the day later, Affleck married *Alias* star Jennifer Garner and their daughter Violet was born six months later in December 2005.

Jennifer credits Marc with making her better balance her life. "He makes me slow down and eat lunch, which I used not to do," she admits. "We have different philosophies. I've been so disciplined. His process is

'Chill, don't kill yourself.' With him I feel like I should relax and slow down. That's a first for me."[15]

After their marriage, Lopez consciously removed herself from the public eye. "It was a choice," she says. "My life for me had become uncomfortable in the way it was affecting my personal life and the people in it, and so I decided that I needed to take a look at that and my own responsibility in that. And I realize there was a way to pull back from it in the way I lived. You don't go out as much. You choose different places to go. You know, if you want to be in those magazines, you can. And if you don't, you don't have to be. It was an adjustment and a compromise, but I found a way to do it."[16]

Her low profile didn't mean Jennifer wasn't working. She produced and starred in *El Cantante*, about Hector Lavoe, known as the King of Salsa and *Bordertown*, inspired by the real life, unsolved murders of Mexican women in Juarez. She also executive produced the reality series *Dancelife* for MTV. Lopez says the series was a "passion project" for her. "Everything that I've been choosing over these past couple of years has to be stuff that I really respond to, that I feel that I can contribute something to. I started my career as a dancer, and so I know what that life is, but I realize that a lot of people don't. The heart of the series . . . is the struggle of loving something so much and doing it and wanting to do it and, at the same time, how hard a life that can be. So that's why I wanted to do it, because I lived it."[17]

But resurrecting career magic proved difficult. *El Cantante* was released in August 2007 and earned Jennifer her best film reviews in years, but the movie only generated $7.5 million at the box office, meaning few people saw the performance. *Bordertown* opened in El Paso, Texas, in 2006 then went straight to video. But Jennifer did receive an award from Amnesty International for bringing the story of the murdered women to film.

Likewise, her music career suffered a slump. In March 2005 she released her fourth studio album (and fifth overall) titled *Rebirth*. The title was symbolic of what Lopez hoped would be a new professional beginning. Although the album produced one modest hit—"Get Right"—sales were tepid and eventually only sold around 600,000 copies in the United States, compared to the almost 3.5 million *On the 6* sold. Her Spanish language album *Como Ama Una Mujer* (How a Woman Loves) was received with a similar lack of interest by fans. Her music career hit its low point in late 2007 with the release of *Brave*. As of December 2007, it was her lowest selling album to date.

On the upside, her autumn 2007 music tour with Marc Anthony was well-received. The couple donated a dollar from every ticket sold to a kids' fitness program called ING Run for Something Better that fights childhood obesity. But the biggest news to come out of the tour was of a personal nature.

In November 2007, on the last night of the tour at Miami's American Airlines Arena Lopez confirmed that the rumors that she was pregnant were in fact true. And she was carrying twins. Her son Max and daughter Emme were born at 12:45 A.M. on February 22, 2008 in Long Island. The babies made their public debut on the March 20 cover of *People*—a privilege for which the magazine paid $6 million. In the issue, Lopez said that it had taken her so long to get pregnant that when her at-home test came back positive, she didn't believe it and took two more tests before she accepted she was really pregnant. She also revealed that she gained nearly 50 pounds to make sure the twins were a good weight at birth. Although they have several assistants, two nurses, and a butler, Jennifer says she and Marc are very hands-on parents, doing the bulk of baby-duty themselves.

Jennifer calls having children a magical time. Looking to the future, she believes she can successfully balance being a wife, mother, and actress. "People ask me, 'Do you think you can have it all?' and you know what? I am like, 'I don't know, I would like to think so.' We will have to wait and see. I think as a person you have to be true to yourself—nobody can tell you what is right for you. I think the problem for women is that we are used to pleasing people, and always wanting for everybody to be happy around us, and sometimes we forget about ourselves. It's important sometimes to think, 'I know what's good for me.'"[18]

And so far, Jennifer's been right more times than not.

NOTES

1. John Millar. "I'm still the same girl who shared a bed with my two sisters in the Bronx." *Sunday Mail*, March 18, 2001. http://www.highbeam.com/doc/1G1–74071525.html.

2. "Interview: Jennifer Lopez—Latino lovely." The News Letter From: May 4, 2001.

3. John Millar. "I'm still the same girl who shared a bed with my two sisters in the Bronx." *Sunday Mail*, March 18, 2001. http://www.highbeam.com/doc/1G1–74071525.html.

4. "Interview: Jennifer Lopez—Latino lovely." The News Letter From: May 4, 2001.

5. John Millar. "I'm still the same girl who shared a bed with my two sisters in the Bronx." *Sunday Mail*, March 18, 2001. http://www.highbeam.com/doc/1G1–74071525.html.

6. David Gardner. "Jennifer Lopez: La Guitara Was So Darned Hot She'd Burn You." *Sunday Mirror*, June 17, 2001. http://www.highbeam.com/doc/1P2–6053243.html.

7. Kate Condon. "I'm Just An Old Fashioned Gal Says Jennifer Lopez." *Daily Record*, August 30, 2001. http://www.highbeam.com/doc/1G1–77696311.html.

8. "Lopez Blames Her Media Image for Hampering Her Film Career." *World Entertainment News Network*, August 8, 2005. http://www.imdb.com/news/wenn/2005–08–08#celeb9.

9. George M. Thomas. "Jennifer Lopez Starring In Her Own Real-Life Cinderella Tale." *Knight Ridder/Tribune News Service*, December 9, 2002. http://www.highbeam.com/doc/1G1–95134462.html.

10. Kate Condon. "I'm Just An Old Fashioned Gal Says Jennifer Lopez." *Daily Record*, August 30, 2001. http://www.highbeam.com/doc/1G1–77696311.html.

11. "J Lo gives her hubby the flick." *The Mirror*, April 25, 2002. http://www.highbeam.com/doc/1G1–85052901.html.

12. Nekesa Mumbi Moody. "Jennifer Lopez splits with husband No. 2 after 8 months of marriage." *AP Worldstream*, June 7, 2002. http://www.highbeam.com/doc/1P1–53482770.html.

13. George M. Thomas. "Jennifer Lopez Starring In Her Own Real-Life Cinderella Tale." *Knight Ridder/Tribune News Service*, December 9, 2002. http://www.highbeam.com/doc/1G1–95134462.html.

14. Paul Fischer. "Jenny: on her rocks." *Sunday Mail*, February 23, 2003. http://www.highbeam.com/doc/1G1–97972571.html.

15. Stephen M. Silverman. "Jennifer Lopez: Marc Makes Me 'Chill.'" *People*, April 13, 2006. http://www.people.com/people/article/0,,1183460,00.html?cid=redirect-articles/.

16. Kathleen Tracy, from in-person press interview.

17. Ibid.

18. Jane Gordon. "Jennifer Lopez—the mother of all divas," *You*. http://www.you.co.uk/pages/you/article.html?in_article_id=511758&in_page_id=1908.

BIBLIOGRAPHY

Adams, Cindy. "Cindy's Romantic Dish." *Good Morning America*, June 12 1998.

Anderson, John. "Fall Movie Preview/November." *Entertainment Weekly*, August 25, 1995, p. 58+.

Anderson, John. "'Money Train' Is Right on Time." *Newsday*, November 22, 1995, p. B5.

Anderson, John. "A Stew of Lust, Diamonds and Contempt." *Newsday*, February 21, 1997, p. B09.

Baldwin, Patrice. "Sex-Crazed Jennifer Lopez Dumped Me! After Only 15 Months, Says Ex-Hubby." *Globe*, January 4, 2000.

Bardin, Brantley. "Woman Of The Year: Jennifer Lopez." *Details*, December 1998. http://members.aol.com/dafreshprinz/jenniferlopez/details1298.htm.

Baumgarten, Marjorie. "Nine Year Itch." *Austin Chronicle*, June 29, 1998.

Béhar, Henri. "On Selena." *Film Scouts*. http://www.filmscouts.com/SCRIPTs/interview.cfm?File=jen-lop.

Bingham, Carolyn. "*Money Train* Wesley Runs Away With It." *Los Angeles Sentinel*, November 22, 1995, p. PG.

Browne, David. *Entertainment Weekly*, June 4, 1999.

Chambers, Veronica, and John Leland. "Lovin' La Vida Loca." *Newsweek*, May 31, 1999, p. 72.

Clark, Mike. "'Anaconda' has Surprising Grip." *USA Today*, October 10, 1997, p. 04D.

"Clooney scores directing hit." *BBC News*. December 23, 2002. http://news.bbc.co.uk/1/low/entertainment/film/2600935.stm.

Condon, Kate. "I'm Just An Old Fashioned Gal Says Jennifer Lopez." *Daily Record*, August 30, 2001. http://www.highbeam.com/doc/1G1-77696311.html.

Corliss, Richard. "¡Viva Selena! The Queen Of Tejano Was Murdered In 1995. Now Hollywood And Her Father Present Their Version Of Her Life." *Time*, March 24, 1997, p. 86.

Cortina, Betty. "The Other Chili Peppers." *Entertainment Weekly*, July 9, 1999.

Covert, Colin. "'Out of Sight' Is One Worth Seeing." *Minneapolis Star Tribune*, June 26, 1998, p. 15E.

"The Crime: Fatal Attraction Fired By The Singer She Adored, Selena's Biggest Fan May Have Turned Deadly." *People*, May 5, 1995, p. 59.

Cunneff, Tom. "Insider." *People*, November 1, 1999.

Daly, Michael. *Talk*, March 2000.

Denerstein, Robert. "Taste Of 'Blood And Wine' Is A Bitter One." *Denver Rocky Mountain News*, March 14, 1997, p. 7D.

"Dream Hampton." *Vibe*, August, 1999.

Duggan, Dennis. "A Rising Latina Star Wows Them in Bronx." *Newsday*, March 20, 1997, A04.

Duncan, Patricia. *Jennifer Lopez*. New York: Macmillan, 1999.

Durchholz, Daniel. *Wall of Sound*, June 1999.

Ebert, Roger. "Lopez a Convincing 'Selena.'" *Minneapolis Star Tribune*, March 21, 1997, p. 06E.

Editorial Staff. *In Style*, June 1999.

Elber, Lynn. "'Selena' Gives A Boost to Hispanics in Films." *The Dallas Morning News*, April 20, 1997, p. 4C.

Feinstein, Howard. "Bob And Jack's Excellent Adventures." *Newsday*, February 2, 1997, p. C08.

Ferrara, Denis, and Diane Judge. "Puff Daddy's Pal?" *Newsday*, November 22, 1998.

"50 Most Beautiful People in The World: Jennifer Lopez, The." *People*, May 12, 1997, p. 124.

Figueroa, Angelo. "Face of Journalism." *National Public Radio*, June 24, 1998.

Fischer, Paul. "Jenny: On Her Rocks." *Sunday Mail*, February 23, 2003. http://www.highbeam.com/doc/1G1-97972571.html.

Fleming, Thomas C. "Bill Cosby/Jennifer Lopez in 'Jack.'" *The Sun Reporter*, August 8, 1996, p. PG.

Frankel, Martha. "Jennifer Lopez Loves To . . . " *Cosmopolitan*, March 1999.

Frankel, Martha. "Love In Bloom." *In Style*, May 1, 1997, p. 196+.

Freeman, Gregory. "TV Can Change the Channel on Hispanic Roles." *St. Louis Post-Dispatch*, September 9, 1994, p. 05C.

Fricke, Jim, and Charlie Ahearn (Editors). *Yes Yes Y'All: The Experience Music Project Oral History of Hip-Hop's First Decade*. Cambridge, MA: Da Capo Press, 2002.

Gardner, David. "Jennifer Lopez: La Guitara Was So Darned Hot She'd Burn You." *Sunday Mirror*, June 17, 2001. http://www.highbeam.com/doc/1P2–6053243.html.

Garner, Jack. "'The Worst Thing to Happen to a Snake since the Creature Handed Eve an Apple." *Gannett News Service*, April 4, 1997, p. arc. http://209.85.173.104/search?q=cache:I61KOW3TJyUJ:www.rochester goesout.com/mov/a/anacon.html+%22The+Worst+Thing+to+Happen+to+a+Snake+since+the+Creature+Handed+Eve+an+Apple%22+garner &hl=en&ct=clnk&cd=2&gl=us.

Gleiberman, Owen. "It Takes a Thief." *Entertainment Weekly*, June 26, 1998, p. 100+.

Glued to the Tube. "Comedy, Drama—Get It? Ralph Farquhar's 'South Central' for Fox Tries to Reflect Life." *Newsday*, April 5, 1994, p. B57.

Gonzales, Michael A. "Jennifer's Many Phases." *Latina*, March 1999. http://www.toppics4u.com/jennifer_lopez/i1.html.

Good Morning America, July 6, 1998.

Green, Tom. "'Money' Cashes In On Stars' Friendly Rivalry." *USA Today*, November 22, 1995.

Guitierrez, Eric. "Busting Boundaries." *Newsday*, March 16, 1997, p. C08.

"Gun found in rapper's car was stolen in Cobb County." *Tampa Bay Online*, December 29, 1999. http://tampabayonline.net/news/news102j.htm.

Handleman, David. "A Diva is Born." *Mirabella*, August 1998. http://members.aol.com/dafreshprinz/jenniferlopez/mirabella0898.htm.

Harris, Mark, ed. "Fall Movie Preview/November." *Entertainment Weekly*, August 25, 1995, p. 58+.

Hasted, Nick. "The Man Who Invented Jack Nicholson." *Independent*, March 10, 1997, p. 12.

Hensley, Dennis. "How Do You Say "Hot" In Spanish?" *Cosmopolitan, 222*, April 4, 1997, p. 190.

Hewitt, Bill, Joseph Harmes, and Bob Stewart. "Up Front: Before Her Time." *People*, April 7, 1995, p. 48+.

Hiltbrand, David. "Picks & Pans: Tube." *People*, August 8,1994, p. 13.

Hiltbrand, David. "Picks & Pans: Tube." People, December 20, 1993, p. 1.

Hobson, Louis B.. "Latino Actors Still Fighting for Respect." *London Free Press*, July 8, 1999.

Hoffman, Adina. "The Serpent's Tale Lacks Bite." *Jerusalem Post*, August 29, 1997, p. 05.

"Interview: Jennifer Lopez—Latino lovely." *The News Letter* (Belfast, Northern Ireland.) May 4, 2001.

"It's Splitsville for Puffy and J.Lo." *CNN*, February 14, 2001.

Ives, Julian Ives. *Mr. Showbiz,* 1997. http://www.lovelylopez.net/mrshowbizinter view.php.

James, Caryn. "'My Family' a warmhearted, ambitious, uneven story." *Minneapolis Star Tribune,* May 19, 1995, p. 19E.

"Jennifer Lopez: She's Proud Of Her 'Bottom Line.'" *USA Today,* July 2, 1998, p. 14D.

"J.Lo by Jennifer Lopez Launches In Stores Nationwide." *PR Newswire,* October 29, 2001.

"J Lo gives her hubby the flick." *The Mirror,* April 25, 2002. http://www.high beam.com/doc/1G1–85052901.html.

Johnson, Hillary. "Beauty Talk: Jennifer Lopez Star Of Selena." *In Style,* April 1, 1997, p. 91+.

Justin, Neal. "The wonderful world of 'Color,'" *Minneapolis Star Tribune,* August 26, 1997, p. 01E.

Karger, Dave. "Biopicked for Stardom." *Entertainment Weekly,* August 9, 1996.

Kitman, Marvin. "The Marvin Kitman Show Take In 'Second Chances.'" *Newsday,* December 2, 1993, p. 109.

Kitman, Marvin. "Welcome To 'Hotel Malibu.'" *Newsday,* August 4, 1994, p. B73.

Lee, Luaine. "Olmos cleared a path for Hispanics." *Minneapolis Star Tribune,* May 17, 1997, p. 04E.

Llorente, Elizabeth. "Her Latina Self." *The Record* (Bergen County, NJ), July 21, 1996, p. l01.

"Lopez Blames Her Media Image for Hampering Her Film Career." *World Entertainment News Network,* August 8, 2005. http://www.imdb.com/news/ wenn/2005–08–08#celeb9.

"Mailbag." *People,* December 21, 1998.

"The Making of Selena." *Hispanic,* March 31, 1997, p. PG.

Maslin, Janet. *The New York Times,* June 4, 1998.

Maslin, Janet. *The New York Times,* June 26, 1998.

Matthews, Jack. "Boy, 10, Doomed to Be Robin Williams." *Newsday,* August 9, 1996, p. B02.

Matthews, Jack. "Though Muted by Dad, 'Selena' Sings." *Newsday,* March 21, 1997, p. B09.

McDivitt, Anita. "New Women's Magazine Uses A Different Tone." *The Dallas Morning News,* June 26, 1996, p. 5C.

McGurk, Margaret A. "This Role Is One Clooney Really Wanted." June 30, 1998, The Cincinnati Enquirer. http://www.Cincinnati.com.

Millar, John. "I'm still the same girl who shared a bed with my two sisters in the Bronx." *Sunday Mail,* March 18, 2001. http://www.highbeam.com/ doc/1G1–74071525.html.

Millar, Sharon. "Father Of J.Lo's Ex Says She Cheated." *The Mirror,* September 20, 2002. http://www.highbeam.com/doc/1G1–91799518.html.

Moody, Nekesa Mumbi. "Jennifer Lopez splits with husband No. 2 after 8 months of marriage." *AP Worldstream*, June 7, 2002. http://www.highbeam.com/doc/1P1–53482770.html.

Morris, Bob. "Could This be Love?" *Talk Magazine*, March 2000. http://beautiful 962.yuku.com/topic/4034/t/Talk-Magazine-March-2000.html.

Morris, Bob. "Line of Fire." *Talk*, March 2000.

"Names in the News." *AP Online*, June 22, 1998.

"Names in the News." *AP Online*, November 14, 1998.

"Networks on Notice Study: Latino TV characters often negative or absent." *Newsday*, September 8, 1994, p. A07.

Ngern-maak, Yaak. "Take Five." *The Nation* (Thailand), June 4, 1998.

"1998: The Year That Was." *Entertainment Weekly*, December 25, 1998, p. 94.

Noguera, Anthony. *FHM*, December 1998. http://www.beyond-beautiful.org/topic/412/t/FHM-December-1998.html.

"On The Rise: Feeling The Heat Money Train's Jennifer Lopez Worries About Copycat Pyros." *People*, December 11, 1995, p. 157.

Page, Clarence. "Networks Tune Out Black Americans." *St. Louis Post-Dispatch*, June 9, 1994, p. 07B.

Page Six, *The New York Post*, May 28, 1998.

Palmer, Martyn. "Sex and the Sisco Kid." *The Mirror*, November 27, 1998. http://www.highbeam.com/doc/1G1–60628260.html.

Palmer, Martyn. *Total Film*, December 1998. http://www.beyond-beautiful.org/topic/3207/t/Total-Film-December-1998.html.

Pener, Degen. "From Here to Divanity." *Entertainment Weekly*, October 9, 1998.

Pener, Degen. "Hey, Nude! Hollywood's Fashion Statement." *Style*, June 1998.

Pennington, Gail. "'Seinfeld' West Has Its Fun With . . . Whatever." *St. Louis Post-Dispatch*, March 27, 1994, p. 08C.

Pennington, Gail. "Hotel Malibu' Checks In." *St. Louis Post-Dispatch*, August 4, 1994, p. 01G.

Poletti, Therese. "Reuters/Variety Entertainment Summary." *Reuters*, December 8, 1996.

Powers, John, and Terry Gross. "'Out of Sight.'" *Fresh Air* (NPR), July 10, 1998.

Press release from Alan Nierob, December 27, 1999.

Proddow, Penny, Marion Fasel, Lisbeth Levine, Robert Ortega, Hollis Brooks, Caroline Schaefer, et al. "Love Stories." *In Style*, February 1, 1998, p. 202+.

Rebello, Stephen. "The Wow." *Movieline*, February 1998. http://members.aol.com/dafreshprinz/jenniferlopez/movieline0298.htm.

Ressner, Jeffrey. "Born to Play the Tejano Queen." *Time International*, March 24, 1997, p. 43

Richmond, Ray. "South Central' Criticized As Depicting Stereotypes." *Los Angeles Daily News*, reprinted in *St. Louis Post-Dispatch*, May 5, 1994, p. 06G.

Roberts, Johnnie L. "Puffy's Crowded Orbit." *Newsweek*, November 8, 1999.

Roberts, Johnnie L, and Allison Samuels. "Under the Gun." *Newsweek*, January 10, 2000. http://www.newsweek.com/id/98453.

Rohan, Virginia. "The Spirit of Selena." *The Record* (Bergen County, NJ), March 20, 1997, p. y01

Roush, Matt. *USA Today*, August 9, 1996.

Rush, George and Joanne Molloy. "Rush and Molloy." *New York Daily News*, May 27, 1999.

Scene + Heard. "News To Amuse: A Star-Studded Review." *In Style*, November 1, 1995, p. 40+.

Schaefer, Stephen. "Plenty Of Clooney In View In 'Out Of Sight' Love Scene." *USA Today*, June 12, 1998, p. 03E.

Schwarzbaum, Lisa. "You've Heard The Song Before 'Selena' Catches The Rhythm But Plays A Tired Tune." *Entertainment Weekly*, March 28, 1997, p. 47.

Schwarzbaum, Lisa. "This Mortal Coil: 'Anaconda' Squeezes Out Some Big B-Movie Moments." *Entertainment Weekly*, April 18, 1997, p. 48+.

Scott Gregory, Sophfronia, Sue Miller, and Natasha Stoynoff. "On the Move: The Right Puff." *People*, October 18, 1999, p. 159.

Seidenberg, Robert. "Legacy Requiem For A Latin Star." *Entertainment Weekly*, April 14, 1995, p. 20.

Self Magazine, October 2000.

Seymour, Gene. "Acting Animated." *Newsday*, December 13, 1998.

Seymour, Gene. "New Paths For Oliver Stone." *Newsday*, October 5, 1997, p. D08.

Silverman, Stephen M. "Ben's Proposal 'Beautiful,' Says Lopez." *People*, November 11, 2002. http://www.people.com/people/article/0,26334,624998,00.html.

Silverman, Stephen M. "Jennifer Lopez: Marc Makes Me 'Chill.'" *People*, April 13, 2006. http://www.people.com/people/article/0,,1183460,00.html?cid=redirect-articles/.

Simon, John. "Tin Cup." *National Review*, 48, September 16, 1996, p. 67.

Sinclair, Tom. "Daddy Oh!" *Entertainment Weekly*, January 7, 2000.

Smith, Kyle, Tom Cunneff, and Champ Clark in Los Angeles; Bob Meadows and Natasha Stoynoff in New York City. "To The Top: Film siren Jennifer Lopez invades the pop scene. But has she conquered Puff Daddy's heart?" *People*, September 13, 1999, p. 71+.

Souhrada, Paul. "Putting On The Glitz." *The Dallas Morning News*, March 29, 1997, p. 10F.

Stoner, Patrick. *Flicks*, April 1997. http://www.whyy.org/tv12/flicksinterviews.html.

Strauss, Bob. "Blood and Guts." *Chicago Sun-Times*. February 16, 1997. http://www.highbeam.com/doc/1P2-4374767.html.

Strauss, Bob. "How a former Fly Girl tackles Selena's memories, Oliver Stone's lunacy and (eeew!) giant killer snakes!" *Entertainment Online*, October 1996.

Strickler, Jeff. "'Money Train' arrives late, then delivers." *Minneapolis Star Tribune*, November 22, 1995, p. 11E.

Tarradell, Mario. "Selena's Power: Cultural Fusion." *The Dallas Morning News*, March 16, 1997, p. 1C.

Tepper, Kirby. "My Family; Mi Familia." *Magill's Survey of Cinema*, June 15, 1995.

Thomas, Bob. "Connie & John: lessons in love. (personal lives of Connie Sellecca and John Tesh)." *Good Housekeeping 218*, March 1, 1994, p. 126.

Thomas, George M. "Jennifer Lopez Starring In Her Own Real-Life Cinderella Tale." *Knight Ridder/Tribune News Service*, December 9, 2002. http://www.highbeam.com/doc/1G1–95134462.html.

Thomas, Karen. "2 Stories of Selena." *USA Today*, March 4, 1997, p. 02D.

Thompson, Douglas. "Jennifer Lopez: The ego has landed." *Sunday Mirror*, November 15, 1998. http://www.highbeam.com/doc/1G1–60646155.html.

"The Triple Threat: Jennifer Lopez is Born." *Famous Entrepreneurs*. http://www.evancarmichael.com/Famous-Entrepreneurs/619/The-Triple-Threat-Jennifer-Lopez-is-Born.html.

Tuck, Stephanie. "Puff & Stuff: He Came, He Saw, He Redecorated." *In Style*, October 1, 1999, p. 388.

Tucker, Ken. "After The Lovin' Connie Sellecca Blows Off An Old Flame In 'Second Chances.'" *Entertainment Weekly*, December 3, 1993, p. 58.

Tucker, Ken. "Summer's Resorts Cheryl Ladd Visit 'One West Waikiki' and Joanna Cassidy Checks Into 'Hotel Malibu,'" *Entertainment Weekly*, August 5, 1994, p. 42.

"25 Most Intriguing People of '99, The" *People*, December 31, 1999.

Usinger, Mike. InfoCulture.com. http://infoculture.cbc.ca/archives/musop/musop_06241999_martinreview.html.

Valdes, Mimi. "Butter Pecan Rican." *Vibe*, June–July, p. 116.

VH1 Fashion Awards, New York City, December 5, 1999.

Vognar, Chris. "'Blood & Wine' Isn't Vintage Stuff." *The Dallas Morning News*, March 14, 1997, p. 5C.

Vognar, Chris. "Selena: Biopic Set Firmly in Ode Mode." *The Dallas Morning News*, March 21, 1997, p. 1C.

Webb, Cynthia L. "Hispanic Films Still Looking For Audience." *Denver Rocky Mountain News*, November 30, 1997, p. 18D.

Welsh, James M. "Jack." *Magill's Survey of Cinema*, September 21, 1996.

West, Dennis. "Filming the Chicano Family Saga." *Cineaste, 21*, December 1, 1995, p. 26.

Westbrook, Bruce. "'Selena' Actress Is on Star Track." *The Dallas Morning News,*
    August 2, 1996, p. 2C.

Williams, Jeannie. "Wishing upon stars to help Democrats." *USA Today,* July 26,
    1996, p. 02D.

"Woman Who Murdered Singer Gets a Sentence of Life in Prison." *New York
    Times,* October 27, 1995. http://query.nytimes.com/gst/fullpage.html?res=
    990CE6D61639F934A15753C1A963958260&scp=2&sq=%22Yolanda+
    saldivar%22&st=nyt.

Wuntch, Philip. "Clooney Tunes Up His Career With New Film." *The Dallas
    Morning News,* June 26, 1998, p. 7.

"You go, J.Lo," *Latina,* June 2001.

Zaslow, Jeffrey. "Straight Talk." *USA Today Weekend,* June 19–21, 1998. http://
    www.usaweekend.com/98_issues/980621/980621talk_lopez.html.

INDEX

About the Author

KATHLEEN TRACY is a Southern California–based journalist. She is the author of over 20 titles, including *Elvis Presley: A Biography* (2006) and *Judy Blume: A Biography* (2007).